Bali Ram

Rhythm by Nature

By Terrie Biggs

ISBN 148401622X
ISBN 13: 9781484016220

Cover by Daniel Biggs, Jr.
Background is fabric from Bali's costume
Website: http://www.danielbiggsphotography.com

Special Thanks

My son Daniel, for introducing me to Bali;
My husband Dan, for his patience and support;
Andrew Stagner, Shala Mattingly, Ted Druch, and
Sukanya Rahman, for their contributions, colorful lives,
and memories;
And Mike Shearer for his editing skills and input.

Table of Contents

Introduction

It is a great honor to me that Bali Ram has allowed me to present his life's memories. After living a most remarkable life, he ended up in Bend, Oregon, U.S.A., as my son's roommate. They worked at the same restaurant/pub where Bali is a prep cook. During the time they shared an apartment together, Daniel would call me and tell me some of the stories Bali had shared with him. We both cried over his poignant experiences with Mother Teresa. They parted as roommates but Daniel, 37 at the time, kept prompting me to go to Bend and interview the youthful, handsome, energetic 76-year-old. Thus began our series of interviews, some in person and many on my phone recorder. The first one was at Daniel's home. That night I invited Bali to dine out with Daniel and me. We decided on Joolz in downtown Bend. A restaurant reviewer described it as "blending the cuisine of eastern Mediterranean with a southwest U.S. flair." Bali held my hand as we walked to the restaurant and it seemed we had formed a strong bond in only a few hours. Daniel, Dan (Sr.) and I had eaten there once and did not understand the menu. We were served about four dishes, all flatbread with different sauces. Bali was an expert, and our dinner was sublime.

The second day of the interview, Bali said he would prepare a Nepalese dinner for us. We were thrilled.

"Okay, Bali. We'll buy the food."

"I'll bring my cooking pots and spices," he said, and then added, "Pick me up about 2 o'clock tomorrow and I will call the farm where I get my meat and they will kill a lamb or goat for us."

Daniel looked at me and we both went, reluctantly, "Ohhh kaaay, Bali." As it turned out the farm was closed that day, and we shopped in town and bought lamb chops, yogurt, cucumbers, rice, cilantro, fresh ginger, etc. Dressed in layers and cooking while wearing a Sherpa hat, Bali prepared the most marvelous, delicious dinner that evening.

Bali preparing our meal in Daniel's house
Photo by Daniel Biggs, Jr.

I returned to Bend to see him perform in a local dance program produced by the Terpsichorean Dance Studio, for which he opened and closed the show. Each performance was about five minutes. His grace and ease of dancing was as natural as water flowing in a river. He had Rhythm by Nature. So I hope my readers are as amazed and beguiled as I am.

Doing an accurate timeline and putting Bali Ram's experiences in date order or according to his age at the time of events and the people he met, has been a challenge for me, which included hours of research. Many times he corrected dates, ages, places, and people as we progressed. He didn't keep playbills or reviews of earlier days of his dancing career which began over 50 years ago. Many events I was not able to verify nor could I refute them. To the best of my ability as a writer, I am recording a man's memories as *he* saw the world and as *he* remembers his life. Could some of it be memories that are not his or not as another remembers? They could be. I have decided that this will be a story based on Bali Ram's life rather than presented as a biography, which has given me liberty to add some dialogue and conjecture about certain events. I was captivated by the way he remembers his life from his paradigm. Before I met Bali, my son Daniel described him to me as Forrest Gump walking in and out of historical events and mingling with famous people, as the movie placed Gump inside the frame with no concept of how significant those people were at the time.

The passion, emotion, and sincerity in which he told me his stories face-to-face, is why I am proceeding with publishing this book, be it entirely factual or some of it creative non-fiction from his memories, I introduce to you *Bali Ram: Rhythm by Nature.*

Prologue

He is an elder dressed impeccably in his white *kurta* (long tunic-like coat), *dhotl* (sari-like loin cloth) and *chappels* (embroidered sandals), brilliant in the sun. He walks along the water's edge in his beloved Kathmandu Valley and finds a shady, grassy spot under an oak tree by the river, flowing lazily like the days of his life at age 76. Still full of energy, wizened by the passing years, his body is still firm and muscular, his skin is light cocoa brown, his eyes twinkle, and his head is now shaven to remove the last sign of losing his beautiful, thick black hair, that at one time hung past his shoulders. He is proud, light on his feet, limber, and still a very handsome man.

As he is seated, reflecting on his life, a golden book appears in his lap. A young, beautiful girl approaches cautiously, in a white *sari*, with rows of bangles on her arm. He looks up and it is Shamina, his 17-year-old daughter. He has tears in his eyes as he takes her hand and beckons her to sit beside him. Shamina begins to watch and to listen as he turns the pages of his golden book of life, glowing in the comfortable shade of the tree. The river eddies and he sees his reflection in the calm water as a child beginning his journey into a life filled with opportunities and events that few men are privilege to, but it came with sacrifices, loneliness, torturous dedication, practice, and ultimately bliss that overwhelmed the struggles.

The pages are turned, one by one, with each page an independent story on its own, and yet combined they form his character, his history, his dreams. Dreams. This is the dream, the vision that a lovely Nepalese man had about the way the story of his life will unfold. So I began crafting each chapter so that the winter of his life will end in honoring him, providing a living history for his children and his country, for the world to remember the famous, classical Indian dancer, Bali Ram.

Bali is a world-wide goodwill ambassador for Nepal and India, which he has honored his entire life through his religion, dress, music, dance, and food.

Bali Ram & Author Terrie Biggs
Photo by Daniel Biggs, Jr.

A Star is Born

Tink. The spoon dropped on the cement floor. The baby went silent. His mother, Shanti, was very nervous because her baby was wailing. She was trying to cool down the milk but by mistake, a spoon dropped on the floor. A few seconds later he began crying again. She picked up the spoon and dropped it again. The baby, named Bali, went silent again.

"Wow. He likes the rhythm, my husband." She tapped the spoon three times. A Nepalese wife could not call her husband by his first name. She must address him as "my husband" or "Bali's father" whereas a husband is able to address his wife by her first name. Tink. Tink. Tink. Her baby, just a few months old, began making cooing sounds. He started smiling and playing with his mother because of the musical sound. So whenever Bali cried, his mother would make the tink tink sound and he would look to see where the soothing tone was coming from. She sang village songs to her child and he would smile and listen. He loved any melodious sound. If he was very fussy, she would take him to the village square while musicians played and drums were vibrating, and it would relax her child and he would fall asleep.

By the time he was eight months he would sit on the floor and move his belly in and out, mimicking dancers, even though he couldn't even stand yet. His mother told Bali, "You loved music from early childhood. You had been born with rhythm by nature."

Temples at Patan, Nepal

Their village of Patan, Nepal, continually had performances. Attracted by the music, the child, just a toddler, would go to the Patan Durbar Square, which was the most important monument of the city. He listened to the music and he would dance by himself. Everybody stopped and said, "Look at this little kid." They put him in the middle while they played instruments, and the village people loved to watch this little fellow who was filled with bliss. The musicians got very excited when they played and Bali danced. He observed the other village dancers doing what was called temple dancing and he mimicked them and learned to move his little body in beautiful poses. People would throw money at him as he twirled and leaped and extended his arms, and lifted his legs.

Bali was the only child born to his mother and father. As much as a he was a great blessing to his mother, he was a disappointment to his father, Man Bahadur, a colonel in the Gurkha Army of Nepal. His father did not like his son dancing or being charmed by music. When Bali began to talk and listen to the music, his father demanded, "You should be a soldier one day." Bali, who had his own dream, would not listen to him. His father began drinking excessively and was very abusive to Bali, grabbing and hitting him many times. If his protective mother interfered, Bali recalled that he saw her thrown across the room. When his father went out, the boy didn't stay home. At night, when his father was drinking, Bali's mother, Shanti Davi Bahadur, would get him out of his father's sight by taking him to a neighbor's home or have him go to bed early.

Born June 6, 1935, his full name was Bali Ram Karkiy Kshtari Bahadur. Patan, the village of his birth, is one of the major cities of Nepal located in the south-central part of Kathmandu Valley in the district of Latipur. Patan is also known as Manigal, and is considered the oldest of all the cities of Kathmandu Valley. It is best known for its rich cultural heritage, particularly its tradition of arts and crafts. It is considered a city of festival and feast, and of fine ancient art of metallic and stone statues. Bali remembers it as being a nice place to spend his childhood. From a child's perspective, he described it: "It was a village but the front of my house was like a big courtyard with temples all around it. There were crowded alleyways, the marketplace, and still more temples." Walking is the easiest method of transportation within the city as the city's core is densely populated. Since pedestrians and vehicles often have to share the same road, traffic congestion is a major problem in Patan.

His parents were Hindu, who comprised over eighty percent of the population, making it the country with the highest percentage of Hindu followers.

Behind their house was a small parcel of land for tending vegetables and raising livestock. His father would farm when he was not working. They grew tomatoes, cauliflower, cabbage, cucumbers, carrots, and cilantro. The livestock included goats and pigs. The house had a big living room, hallway, and two bedrooms. In the middle of the main living area floor was the stove for cooking and it was the source of heat for the family. Meals were prepared with care and reverence, filling the house with aromas of curry spices and freshly chopped vegetables from the garden.

Bali's neighbor, who made goat cheese, had four children, and one day one of the boys asked Bali, "We're going to India to market our cheese. We will be there for three months. Would you like to go with us?"

"I don't know. You'll have to ask my mother," Bali replied.

Bali's friend went to Shanti, Bali's mother, and asked, "We are going to India. Can we take Bali with us?"

His mother thought for a moment and said, "Yes. I'll come with you." She knew the relief it would bring to get Bali away from his father for three months. However, Bali's father did not want her to leave but, of course, he had no objection if Bali went. Reluctantly, she said goodbye to her beloved son, not knowing at the time that his destiny would be shaped by letting him go.

At seven and a half Bali started for India with the neighbors. He described his companions' mode of transportation as "a house over a cart pulled by four cows, like oxen." When they arrived in Calcutta, Bali had never seen so many buildings. He was mesmerized by the hustle and bustle of a big city. Across the street from where they stopped was a big park with a lot of people and it was bustling with activity.

Bali said, "What's going on there? We should go see."

His companions said, "Yes!" and they parked by the side of the road and they all entered the park. It was muggy, sticky, and smelly! Bali couldn't see because he was only a small boy, so he went underneath, between the legs of the people, up to the front to see what was happening. All sweaty and dirty, wearing a torn T-shirt, Bali forced himself between a man and a woman who seemed to be the center of attention and were engaged in a discussion. Bali looked right in their faces. He didn't know what language they were speaking because he was Nepalese. Young Bali was totally unaware that they were shooting an Indian movie and a scene was in progress, while the crowd gathered to see the hero and heroine.

They were making a movie in the Hindi language which he could not understand. The two actors stopped their conversation and began laughing while looking at the boy who wedged his way between them. Then Bali heard somebody shouting, something like, "Cut it out," or "Stop making the movie. Who's this kid?" The director sent one of the British men to talk to Bali. The man was six foot tall, had blond hair and blue eyes. He was talking the dialect of Dakar and Bali didn't know what he was saying. Finally the man spoke to Bali in his own tongue and Bali was amazed and said, "My God! You speak my language?"

The Brit answered, "Yes. I am Nepalese."

"I am Nepalese, also," Bali replied.

The man asked, "What is your father's name?"

"His name is Man Bahadur."

"What's his full name?"

Bali answered him.

"Well then, I know your dad because we were in the same regiment in Nepal." The Brit was born in India and joined the army of Bali's country when he was a teenager.

"Can you imagine that? How the connection happened?" Bali asked me.

"This was a splendid example of serendipity, of extraordinary circumstance," I answered. "Tell me what happened next."

The director liked Bali right away and he talked with the Brit. The tall man interpreted the director's message, "Would you like to work in the movie?"

Bali asked, "Me?"

"Yeah, you," his new acquaintance replied.

Without hesitation, Bali responded, "Will they pay me?"

The Brit burst out laughing and said, "You're smart. You're smart."

"Well, I don't know what smart means, but yes, if they pay me, I will work."

So he went back to the director and said, "He's very bright. If you pay him he will work," and they all laughed.

The director said, "Okay."

Bali introduced his new friend, Desmond Doig, to the family he came to the park with, and Doig took down his address in Nepal along with his parents' names. Even though Doig and Bali's father were not well acquainted during their years in the army, Doig would stay at their home when he was doing a story in Nepal and he became friends with Bali's family. A lifelong association between Bali and Desmond Doig began. Bali had no clue how prominent Doig was until he had grown a bit older. At that realization, he told himself, "Oh my God, he was the newspaper boss. Editor of the newspaper."

Desmond Doig by George Cserna

Doig was the assistant editor and roving reporter for the *Calcutta Statesman*, an English language daily newspaper. Calcutta, India, was renamed Kolkata.

Born August 17, 1921, in Allahabad, India, to British parents, Doig received the equivalent of a high school diploma in Kurseong, India. He served in the Indian Army from 1939 to 1947 in the Fifth Royal Gurkha Rifles of Nepal, where he met Bali's father. He became captain and received the Africa Star and Italy Star. His many talents included artist, writer, and architectural designer. From 1967 he was editor of *JS* a fortnightly magazine for young people. Notable assignments included: 1959, the first reporting from Nepal, Bhutan, and Nagaland, the flight of the Dalai Lama into India; 1962, the Indo-Chinese War; 1964, the assassination of Bhutanese prime minister, Jigme Dorji, and the execution of the assassins. He introduced the world to Mother Teresa. The artistry of his sketches resulted in published books of his drawings. Doig spoke fluent Nepalese and Sherpa along with Hindi. Bali so beautifully described him: "He had an Indian soul in a western body." Could one say more to honor Doig's love of India and Nepal?

The families kept in touch while Bali was growing up. Bali would stay with Doig occasionally on school vacations. Doig arranged a passport for Bali and took him with him to New York to visit his family. One day Doig's family went to a party and Bali stayed at the Manhattan apartment. The Doigs had a collection of Indian records, and Bali was playing them on the turntable. He was dancing and moving his body to the rhythm of the music. After the record was over the time had slipped away and it was in the middle of the night, when Doig came out of the curtains and was clapping and "making a noise" which startled Bali so much that Bali fell to the floor crying.

Doig picked him up and said, "I am sorry that I scared you. I have been watching you. Well, we have discovered something today. I was worried about you, Bali. I didn't know how you will survive, or what to do with you. Now I know."

"Yeah, what is that?"

"You like to dance. I have discovered you. It was so beautiful. You should be a classical dancer. So, I'll put you in the academy."

Doig set it up for Bali to go to an Indian dance academy and thus the incredible career of this child was about to change his life and destiny forever.

A Walk with Gandhi

Twice each day Mohandas Karamchand Gandhi took a brisk walk. The poet Ragindranath Tagore attached "Mahatma" to his name, meaning "Great Soul" which is what he is commonly called. In 1930, Gandhi left his ashram at Ahmedabad on foot to the sea with civil resistance volunteers. This was the beginning of civil disobedience in the manner of non-violent defiance of the British administration as an act of defiance of the British monopoly on the sale of salt, and brought into action the surge for complete independence from British rule in India. Before embarking on the 240-mile journey Gandhi sent a letter to the Viceroy himself, forewarning their plans of civil disobedience which read:

"If my letter makes no appeal to your heart, on the eleventh day of this month I shall proceed with such co-workers of the Ashram as I can take, to disregard the provisions of the Salt Laws. I regard this tax to be the most iniquitous of all from the poor man's standpoint. As the Independence movement is essentially for the poorest in the land, the beginning will be made with this evil."

As promised, on March 12, 1930, Gandhi and 78 male activists "of truth and resolution" started their 23 day journey. Women weren't allowed to march because Gandhi felt women wouldn't provoke law enforcers like their male counterparts, to react violently to non-violence.

The two-mile long procession was watched by every resident along the journey. On April 6, Gandhi raised a grain of salt and declared, "With this, I am shaking the foundations of the British Empire."

Gandhi's plan appealed to people in every region, class, religion, and ethnicity. The successful campaign led the British government to imprison over 60,000 people for making or selling salt without a tax. The British opened fire on the unarmed crowd and shot hundreds of demonstrators. Gandhi was arrested in his sleep on the night of May 4th, 1930.

In 1936 people began labeling the movement "Gandhism" of which he did not approve, as he explained, "There is no such thing as 'Gandhism,' and I do not want to leave any sect after me. I do not claim to have originated any new principle or doctrine. I have simply tried in my own way to apply the eternal truths to our daily life and problems...The opinions I have formed and the conclusions I have arrived at are not final. I may change them tomorrow. I have nothing new to teach the world. Truth and non-violence are as old as the hills."

Bali's mother took her son to Gandhi's ashram by the seashore to see the man she, like millions of Indian and Nepalese under the British rule, admired and loved. Bali says of his encounter with a great leader, "My mom and I were walking on the beach early in the morning. I was just seven years old, and I got so bored, I wondered, 'Who this old man?' I thought, 'His legs like a twig they are so skinny.'" The old man in front of him was using his walking stick. "I said to myself that if I take his stick from him, I will play horsie on it. I began running and I ran through this old man's legs and grabbed his stick, but the old man won't let go of stick and he ran after me and somebody took the picture."

The only photo of Bali's mother to the right of Gandhi's head.

"Have you seen the photo of Bali with Gandhi?" Shala Mattingly asked me. Bali treasures the photo and she remembered it from the time she first met Bali and he showed it to her while they were both in dance academies in New Delhi about 1960.

Mattingly thought it was the only picture Bali has of his mother, who is in the background to the right of Gandhi's head. She thought that his mother visited Gandhi occasionally to get away from her abusive husband. I told Mattingly that I also located a second photo.

This photo has appeared with an internet article about the Salt March which took place in 1930, in other places in the internet, and in books from what I have been told. A date has not been established when it was taken. Many people have asked who the child is in the photograph. This is one of the events I have been unable to substantiate except for Bali's vivid recollection of that day. He said that a friend of his mother's took the picture. He has carried the photograph with him most of his life, which would conclude that it was taken about 1942.

The "Quit India" movement was launched in 1942, demanding immediate self-rule. Gandhi, Nehru, and other political leaders were arrested and imprisoned the morning after the All-Asia Congress Committee session, when the "Quit India" resolution was adopted, calling for the immediate dissolution of British rule.

Gandhi was the preeminent leader of Indian nationalism in British-ruled India. Employing non-violent civil disobedience, Gandhi led India to independence and inspired movements for non-violence, civil rights and freedom across the world. On January, 30, 1948, Gandhi was shot and killed while he was walking to a platform from which he was to address a prayer meeting. The world mourned his passing and India got her independence from British rule with assistance of a skinny old man who took walks twice a day, with legs like a twig.

Rhythm by Nature

Every moment that Bali danced he enjoyed, except for the painful learning process. As a young boy he watched the villagers perform their own style of dancing. It was not a classical dance, or one style, it was folk dancing. People got together in the evening by the fire and danced and sang. There was always music and drumming. Young Bali loved to watch his village people dancing and he began mimicking their movements with a rhythm uncanny for a young boy. He had an innate, a rhythm by nature. His mother made his costumes when he danced formally in the village for festivals or for weddings. It was village dance, and people would throw money at him and applaud his dancing.

It takes many painfully, disciplined years to learn the dances, and he had begun very young. When people noticed that he could dance, they would come and drag him out of his house and try to put bells on him. At first, he resisted the five pound, anklet bells. He spent many hours practicing every day. Just dancing, dancing. There were times that, as a boy, he thought he was going to die he was so exhausted, and it was so painful on his bare feet, swollen and bloody with blisters. His mother soaked his feet in salt water, and then tenderly rubbed mustard oil on them. The next day he could barely walk. He used to cry, wondering if his feet would ever heal, whether the pain and agony would ever go away. As a young village dancer, he had not learned the proper way to hit the ground.

He attended school in Nepal until Doig sponsored him in a dance academy. In 1958 Doig brought sixteen year old Bali with him to Calcutta and introduced him to Indrani Rahman, one of India's foremost classical Bharata Natyam and Odissi artists, who became the first Miss India. Indrani's mother was an American-born dancer who introduced India's classical dances to many in the U.S. Born to an American family in Michigan in 1893, Esther Sherman changed her name to Ragini Devi after discovering classical Indian dance which she described as an act of worship. Clothed in *saris,* with a vermillion mark on her forehead, she darkened her skin, and convinced reporters in 1926 that she was a native of India.

Indrani's daughter, Sukanya Rahman, a third generation dancer, and author of *Dancing in the Family,* recalled the time that her mother met Bali. "Bali's looks and talent in dance brought him to my mother's attention and to Delhi. She arranged for him to study Bharata Natyam with Sikkil Ramaswamy Pillai at Triveni Kala Sangam in Delhi. She presented Bali in her performances and also partnered with him."

Triveni Kala Sangam

The academy taught classical Indian dancing, which is the study and interpretation of *Bharata Natyam Mudras*, which are hand gestures to mime the meaning of a song or Indian mythology. Each gesture has a particular meaning and may vary in interpretation depending on the school in which they were taught.

Bali Ram demonstrating *Mudras*
Photo by Desmond Doig

The *Bharata Natyam* is a classical dance from South India dating back to 10,000 B.C. In ancient times it was performed as a court dance. Hindu temples have ancient sculptures based on these dance postures giving this style a common name of temple dancing. *Bharata Natyam* is considered a "fire dance" as dancers resemble the movements of a dancing flame. It is considered a dance of yin and yang – Lasya, the graceful lines and movement of the female, and the dance of Shiva, with elements of masculinity. A perfect balance.

Bharata Natyam is the manifestation of the celebration of the eternal universe through the celebration of the beauty of the material body. The movements and hand gestures were designed to bring spiritual enlightenment to the audience. They are a form of grace and beauty, telling ancient stories with the body, accompanied by music.

Bali compared the hand gestures to American Sign Language in that the hands gestures have the same meaning. All dancers know by the posture or movement of the hands what it means. Thousands of people in villages can watch and understand the language of the hands and they can laugh or boo or respond according to the gestures.

Triveni Kala Sangam is a self-supporting cultural and arts complex and education center in New Delhi, founded by Sundari K. Shridharani. Triveni, as it is commonly referred, contains four art galleries, a chamber theater, outdoor theater, open air sculpture gallery, besides this it runs its various arts, music and dance classes. The name *Triveni Kala Sangam* literally means "confluence of arts." It started in one room above a coffee house in Connaught Place, Delhi, with two students under noted artist K. S. Kulkarni in 1951. Bali began his training while the school was still located at Connaught Place.

American architect, Joseph Allen Stein, designed the multi-purpose complex. Construction began around 1957 and Bali and the students moved to the new facility. It was full of life and light, and it was state-of-the-art. Art Heritage Gallery was founded in 1977, by noted theater personality, Roshen Alkazi, wife of theatre director Ebrahim Alkazi. It was a period before a host of commercial art galleries opened up across Delhi, and especially in South Delhi, even then Triveni managed to maintain its non-commercial approach to art.   Roshan ran the gallery for over 40 years till her death in 2007.

Today the Triveni complex contains four art galleries, and a basement gallery. The complex also houses Triveni Chamber Theater, Triveni Garden Theater (an outdoor theater), Triveni Sculpture Court (an open air sculpture gallery), students' hostels, classes in various dances and music forms, classes in painting and photography, and there is a potted plant nursery, and a book shop.

Bali studied there for four or five years. He did not sleep there. He stayed in his rental house in New Delhi. There was a resting place at the academy for the students to stay while waiting for classes. School began at 8 a.m. with one hour lunch breaks, a couple of bathroom breaks, and he got home about 5:30 in the evening. It was strict and disciplined. If a person did not have discipline, they would have to leave because the teachers would not tolerate them. In his class there were about fifteen or twenty students. Sometimes he would practice on Sunday for a concert with his teacher. It was a large hall with high ceilings where they danced and the dancers could stand up on each other and jump in the new academy, unlike the original facility in Connaught Place which was small, which he said was like a storage room.

Bali thought that there were six dance teachers.

The head teacher was Sikkil Ramaswamy Pillai, who was about 84 years old when Bali attended, and was from South India. Bali said that Pillai was a very beautiful person. When he walked into the room Bali was mesmerized by his grace and confidence, and wanted to be like him. Pillai had a hypnotic effect on Bali when he demonstrated the dance and Bali wished it would have gone on forever, it was so beautiful.

"Bali, are you paying attention?" Pillai would scold.

"Oh, I am sorry, sir. Yes. Yes, sir." The old man didn't know that his presence made Bali go deeper, beyond the dancing, like he was doing it himself. In spite of his age, Pillai's expressions and his movement of dance had the elegance and grace of a young man. Pillai was devoted to one thing, his dance. Nothing else mattered to him.

Bali already had built up calluses before he attended the academy from his years of dancing. Achieving balance was very important. He said that he must wear the bells in order to pose correctly, often lifting one leg up, and he attained balance with the bells.

There were no drums in the daily classes. Pillai used a small stick of wood about two and a half inches thick, and he would beat that for the rhythm in class. The sound was like a castanet. When there was a concert, the whole percussion would be there. It was too expensive for the whole percussion to play daily for the classes. Concerts were every three or four days, or at least once a week for the theaters in town: movie theater, football stadium, playgrounds, university theater schools, elementary, high schools and colleges.

Bali loved to dance with percussions, and he felt

a high as though he was coming out of his body "in top of seventh heaven," he said. The concerts were good practice for the students. Bali explained, "Indian dance was started by Shiva in the very beginning of time of humanity when the gods and goddess used to dance. Shiva had the rhythm. It is a difficult task to do Indian dance, that's why foreigners don't usually adopt it. It's not play, it is devotion. When you do it over the years, it possesses you. All the rhythm goes into your head and your body. Indian classical dance is temple dancing because Lord Shiva started it. He knew how to dance and how to balance harmony between sage and saint. He was the controller of the rhythm. Shiva was the first dancer - a male dancer - and then women started doing it." It is now about even between male and female performers, and he said that everybody dances whether it is classical or not. They love to dance in India. "Whether it is folk dance, or hootchy-cootchy, they just move their bodies. They have a lot of rhythm.

"The Indian way of teaching class was incredible. You have no time even to talk to your own classmates. Two or three teachers are present right there. In the classroom you can't even whisper or talk. Very disciplined."

Summer breaks were in June and July, lasting about six weeks, and then the rainy season began. School would commence when the rainy season ended. Bali stayed with Pillai one summer in South India in Addiyar. He spent most school breaks with Doig in Calcutta, and sometimes they would go to America. Doig's wife and children lived in New York City. U.S.A.

Bali also went to summer school while he was in New York to learn and practice English.

Doig's parents had a home in Kent, England, where his family would spend Christmas. Doig would return to Calcutta for work and when Bali went back to India, he would stay with Doig until school resumed. Bali loved and admired his sponsor. "Desmond was very beautiful soul. His family was a very holy family to me because they adopted me as part of their family and took care of the all the expenses for me. I spent winters with them dancing and learning English. At that time English was the second language in India, but now it has become first language. Everybody speaks English because India is a melting pot. The Indian movies are spoken in English."

There were times during the years of training that Bali wanted to quit. Bali said, "At times I regretted it. I thought that this should have been warning to me to get the heck out of here! But it was part of learning process.

"As long as I'm taking dance classes, I have to do that. But, when I come on the stage, people couldn't get enough of it. The audience would call, 'Once more! Once more! Once more! More, more, more, Bali Ram.' I didn't realize I was that good." It was then that he knew the agony, calluses, and discipline were all worth it.

Bali recalled, "When the training process was over at my academy, everything came much easier. Then I know what to dance, how much dance, how much strength I can put in. I know how to jump and land. I can dance for eight hours and never go..." He breathed heavily in and out indicating being winded. "Never out of breath."

His father did not have to speak with or tolerate what he considered his failure of a son while Bali was in school. "I wish he could have seen me practicing in school," Bali said, "Maybe he would say, 'My God, all these bells on the kid's legs...'" But he never received a kind word from his father or any sense of pride in Bali's accomplishments.

His Journey Had Begun

After graduation, Rukmini Davi, founder of the Kalaksheta Academy in Besant Nagar, wrote a letter to Doig when he first danced in Calcutta. It was published in his flyers. She said, "Congratulations to Bali Ram. He will be a great dancer." The letter is in his album of dance flyers.

When he was 17 or 18, Bali's mother said, "Let me see your hand."

"Why? Is there something wrong with my hand?" Bali asked.

"There is nothing wrong. Every child is born with his hand closed when he comes into this world. Slowly, as they grow, their hands open and the words from God begin to form. He writes a life for you. When the hand is fully opened to receive God's message, a child's journey and destiny begin. You have fully opened your hand to accept God's words. Your journey has begun."

Shala Mattingly

Shala Mattingly and Bali were studying at two different colleges of music and dance that were down the road from each other in New Delhi. She was in the government college of music and dance called Bharatiya Kala Kendra academy, currently referred to as Kathak Kendra, studying *Kathak*, which is known as the classical styles of dance of Northern India. Bali was studying Southern Indian dance. She attended her academy for two years. Mattingly was a professional dancer in England trained in tap, ballet, and character dance before she went to India. She went there specifically to study dance which she had seen in London in 1956. She moved to India in 1958 to Bombay, and then relocated in Delhi in 1960. She was the first non-Indian to be awarded a Government of India scholarship to study *Kathak*. After her training, she travelled around India lecturing and performing to the Indian people on their own art form. She was awarded a second scholarship by Indian Council of cultural Relations.

Bali appeared at her academy one day. The students at her academy visited people at Bali's and vise versa. Bali was also performing with Indrani and her company at that time. Mattingly described Bali as good looking and slender, with full, wavy hair that turned up in curls at the nape of his neck.

Over the years he partnered with Indrani, they both looked exotically beautiful on stage and dramatically exciting to watch. However, Indrani's great beauty was matched by a great temper and a dominant personality. The first time Mattingly saw Bali dance with Indrani was in New Delhi around 1960. After the performance Mattingly went backstage to meet them but was not successful as everyone was running in all directions away from a raging Indrani as she berated stagehands for not cooperating adequately during the performance! Later, while living in New York, Indrani and Shala had a perfectly amicable relationship and helped each other out whenever they could.

Mattingly started dancing as a child in Wimbledon, which was her home in England. She was a shy child, and told me, "My mother didn't know what a monster she was creating when she sent me to dancing school." In 1956, at age 18, she was working as a singer and dancer in *Cabaret* in London when she saw posters around London advertising Ram Gopal and his company of musicians, singers and dancers from India. There was a magnificent photograph of him on the poster. "The poster was saffron color. I remember every time I saw this color, my heart would leap. Finally one day I read what he was all about and saw his photo and I had to go and see him. He was at the Royal Festival Hall in London." Before the curtain went up Mattingly said she was in love. She could smell the incense and she heard the Indian musical instruments tuning up, and the ankle bells behind the curtain. "Once the curtain went up, that was it." That's when she decided she had to go to India to study, but her parents wouldn't let her go until she was 21, which was the legal age in England at that time.

As soon as she was 21, off she went. She didn't have the means or the money to go on her own, but she used to take theatrical papers in London called *The Stage,* which is still going strong, and she found an advertisement stating that performing artists - cabaret artists - were required for India. She applied and she went to India with three other girls. Two girls were from Scotland, and one from London.

Mattingly was working on a year's contract and during that period she found her first teacher in Bombay. Two years later she moved to Delhi where she met Bali. While in India, she met an American man, Joseph Levine, and he became *Raja* later on. She introduced him to her teacher, and he started training with him, also. Levine and Mattingly began performing together around India. He went back to New York and she returned to

England, where Ram Gopal asked her to work with him in London. It was so extraordinary for her to have her idol call upon her. Gopal was in his mid 50's at that time, and the interest in Indian dance in England had faded. He talked about a lot of things, but things never actually happened.

Shala Mattingly & Bali

When Mattingly set aside her dancing, she became a leading specialist in past life regression therapy. She is not active in her practice at this time. Here is a description from her website: *Certified in clinical, forensic and regressive hypnosis, she has maintained a professional practice in the heart of Manhattan since 1981. She travels internationally lecturing and conducting workshops for public and professional groups and is a frequent guest on radio and television talk shows. For many years she has been a featured speaker at major health expositions and has taught at The Learning Annex in New York City. London born Shala F. Mattingly is currently preparing a book detailing some of the fascinating case histories she has encountered in her practice. Additionally, her work is featured in three published books: "Earthly Cycles" by Ramon Stevens, "Returning From the Light" by Brad Steiger, "Psychic New York" by Patricia Collins, as well as two new books to be published within the next year. Shala F. Mattingly is a member of The International Association of Counselors and Therapists.*

Mattingly has been very kind and helpful in supplying background on Bali while they were performing in India and in New York and has a better handle on dates than Bali. He doesn't seem to have a perception of time. She lost track of Bali for about 25 years, and now they talk a few times a month.

Miracles of Mother Teresa

Lord, Make me an instrument of Your peace,
Where there is hatred, let me sow love;
Where there is injury, pardon;
Where there is doubt, faith;
Where there is despair, hope;
Where is darkness, light;
And where there is sadness, joy.
O divine Master, grant that I may not
So much seek to be consoled as to console;
To be understood as to understand;
To be loved as to love;
For it is in giving that we receive;
It is in pardoning that we are pardoned;
And it is in dying
That we are born to eternal life.

St. Francis of Assisi

"We're going to Calcutta," Doig announced to Bali at the graduation ceremony.

"Why Calcutta? Why not New York?" Bali had traveled with Doig back and forth from India to New York.

"You have to meet a nun. She's a Catholic nun."

Very confused due to his country's traditions of prearranged marriages, Bali asked Doig, "Why? Are you making an arranged marriage?"

Doig burst out laughing, "Oh, no. You just have to meet her."

"But, why?"

"I don't know," Doig countered. "You might be able to help her."

"Which way help her?"

"You should meet her. Don't give me lip." He was like a father to Bali. "You are arguing too much. I cannot explain this to you. It's just happening, and you have to come with me."

"Okay," Bali consented.

Bali went to Calcutta with Doig and the next day he was introduced to the nun. Bali described her as white skinned and dressed in white. She was tiny. The woman looked at Bali and said, "Well, you are a very handsome young man. Would you like to help me? I'm Mother Teresa."

"How can I help you?"

"With my work. I need some help. Young people like you…"

Bali agreed to help this tiny woman. At that time she was in the beginning of her work on the streets of Calcutta among the leper people. Bali described his experience while helping Mother Teresa. He removed their clothes, bathed them, and he put the clothes back on their ravaged bodies. For some of the people, food had to be ground up because they did not have the aperture, only a hole. The ground up food was put into the hole in their throats until they gestured that they were full. They could not talk. Bali said, "It was horrible, horrible fate."

MotherTeresa wrote in her diary that her first year was fraught with difficulties. She had no income and had to resort to begging for food and supplies. Teresa experienced doubt, loneliness and the temptation to return to the comfort of convent life during these early months. In 1950 Teresa received Vatican permission to start a congregation that would become the Missionaries of Charity. Its mission was to care for, in her own words, "the hungry, the naked, the homeless, the crippled, the blind, the lepers (Hansen's Disease), all those people who feel unwanted, unloved, uncared for throughout society, people that have become a burden to the society and are shunned by everyone." Her motivating force as told to Doig was, "When I cleanse the wounds of the poor, I am cleansing the wounds of Christ."

Mother Teresa Photo by Teki

It began as a small order with 13 members in Calcutta. Ultimately her charity work included nuns running orphanages, AIDS hospices and charity centers world-wide, caring for refugees, the blind, disabled, aged, alcoholics, the poor, the homeless, and victims of floods, epidemics, and famine.

Desmond Doig was the first journalist to write about Mother Teresa when she first arrived in Calcutta and covered her miraculous work for 27 years while he worked at the *Calcutta Statesman*. In 1978 he published the collection of the articles about his dear friend in his book, *Mother Teresa, Her People and her Work*. Doig was intimately acquainted with this tiny woman born of Albanian parents in Yugoslavia in 1910 who was sent to Calcutta from Dublin, Ireland, where she taught geography in Calcutta at a Catholic school and was principal of the school before she took her vows. In 1947 India gained its independence from British rule and she became an Indian citizen in 1948. She asked to live apart from the cloister and began with one Bengali girl in 1949. October 1950 marked the date of the founding of the Mother House in Calcutta, which eventually spread throughout India providing medication, bandages and food. Home of the Pure Heart was provided for her by the city of Calcutta which was a converted Hindu temple and it allowed the stricken to die with dignity based on their religious rituals. "A beautiful death," she said, "is for people who lived like animals to die like angels—loved and wanted."

The converted temple, called *Kalighat* - Home for the Dying, was in one of the most congested areas of the already overcrowded city. There was a labyrinth of narrow lanes, middle-class houses, slums dwellings, shops, pilgrims' rest houses and *ghats* where the dead were cremated.

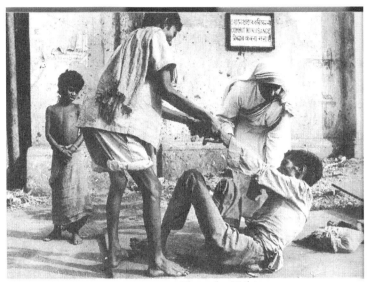

Photo by Teki

On the program "Oprah and Deepak Chopra in India," Chopra described India as full of paradoxes and contradictions. He told Oprah that India is an "assault in the senses — the colors, the textures, fragrances…India had a violent past and India is sustained by its spiritual essences. It has absorbed foreigners and made them Indians," as transpired with Mother Teresa when she took on citizenship.

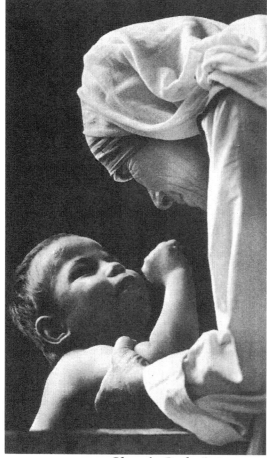

Photo by Raghu Rai

Oprah added that she felt it was chaotic with an underlying flow of calmness. Inquiring from Chopra what he meant by spiritual essences, he said so beautifully, "Living historical connection to its great teachers, about time and space and causality and karma and connection to the spirit. The unbounded consciousness and it has sustained this country through thousands of years."

Doig described Calcutta as, "Rich and poor. A millionaire family bearing expensive gifts in gold tissue. Devotees in white cotton leading goats to sacrifice.

Saffron-robed yogis with piled hair and extravagant cast marks vermillion on their foreheads. Beggars. Tourists. Troubadours singing devotional songs, plaintive, like sighs set to music. Balloon men almost airborne. Skeins of students. Mendicants. And now, strangely, nuns in blue-bordered white saris.

"There is always festive confusion particularly in its shanty shops which sell everything from fruit and carved wood to brass cooking pots and fresh fish and caged birds. Over all is a blue mist of funeral pyres, and the smell of incense mingles with the smell of death. Boisterous life and calm acceptance of death is characteristic. Numerous funeral processions nudge shoppers and high-spirited children playing in the road."

In his Mother Teresa book, Doig said so eloquently, "Prayer was the subject of one of our many discussions. I must feel eternally grateful for all the time that Mother Teresa has allowed me just as I must feel forever guilty at having taken up so much of it. No one I know who has ever met Mother Teresa, for however short a while, has been unmoved by the experience. For some, it has meant a completely new way of life; for me, it has been one of the most extraordinary experiences of a fairly eventful life. She has taught me to see, not merely to look, to appreciate, not merely to understand, and she has consolidated whatever faith I had. I can think of no one I would like to have with me more when I am in real need or when my time is up than Mother Teresa because, for me, she has, I suppose unconsciously, built up a powerful vocabulary of understanding, which even as a non-practicing Christian I can comfortingly use."

In the parlor of the Mother House were three boards, each displaying the philosophies of her work.

Two boards contained photographs and her prayers were printed below photographs. One illustrated what the requirements were of the congregation, to "walk in the footsteps of Jesus." Another board with photographs had her prayers below which read, "Make us worthy, Lord, to serve our fellow-men through the world who live and die in poverty and hunger. Give them through our hands, this day their daily bread, and, by our understanding, love, peace and joy."

Therefore, it is easy to understand why Doig wanted Bali to be exposed to such grace and compassion at a young age, before Doig introduced Bali to the world. I believe this experience set Bali's moral compass for life.

Bali described his experience with Mother Teresa. "She was Yugoslavian. Dressed in white *sari*, Indian wear, and she had border, blue border all around the *sari*, all around the edges, but white *sari*. That's what she wore in India."

Then he described what he called a miracle. "I noticed one thing at night that when we put bandages on them, the next day we opened (the bandages), the seepage stopped. Normally, it took six to seven to eight months to heal, but no longer seepage. Her prayer was very strong. Prayer. It was incredible. We didn't have any Lysol. We didn't have any Clorox. We didn't have anything, just the soap. Plain Indian soap. We had no antibiotic. No nothing. Leprosy is very contagious and nothing happen to me. I was bandaging them and cleaning, and taking them nude in the shower with me because they cannot hold on to anything. It's like they are a baby. I had to put them on the floor, put soap on them, everywhere - face, and everything - and then shower them, clean them, wipe them, bring them out, clothe them, and put them in the bed. For six months I did that."

After six months of serving the unfortunate victims, Mother Teresa said, "I have to ask you one favor, Bali Ram"

"What is it?"

She looked at him with her head cocked to one side, as she said, "I want you to dance for me, for my cause, to bring some money so we can be more self-sufficient."

"Yes, I can do that for you."

The Governor of the Indian state of Uttar Pradesh came to the show in Calcutta. Sarojini Naidu was a distinguished poet, renowned freedom fighter and one of the great orators of her time. She was famously known as *The Nightingale of India*. This distinguished woman was the first Indian woman to become the President of the Indian National Congress and the first woman to become the governor of a state in India.

The fundraising performance was held in an English club, the New Empire Theater, which had a large hall. No Indians had been allowed into the club while under British rule. At Mother Teresa's invitation, Governor Naidu was granted entrance. After two days, the money piled up and was on a table where Mother Teresa and the governor were seated talking to Bali.

Mother Teresa said, "Bali, take some money."

"What?"

"Well, you performed for two days. You have to go back to New Delhi and you need some money to go back."

Bali refused, saying, "No. I'm okay." After arguing with her and Governor Naidu, Bali said that he didn't feel it was respectful to argue with Mother Teresa, so he said, "Okay. " He reached out, picked up one Indian penny, and he put it in his pocket and he declared, "That's it. No more."

Mother Teresa said, "Ah, you're so stubborn," and she rose, walked slowly towards Bali, facing him. She put her hands on his head and said, "I bless you with all my heart and so wherever you will be on this planet earth, I shall be with you."

Bali was so touched by her blessing and told her, "Mother Teresa, *that* I accept. That's the biggest gift you can ever give me." She was very happy and Bali bowed down to her, and she blessed him again. The governor was clapping and rejoicing in the unselfish nature of Bali Ram and the lifetime grace that Mother Teresa bestowed on him.

Eventually, as described in Doig's book, with statistics around 1976, the Missionaries of Charity had 61 foundations in India and 28 abroad. They had 81 schools, 335 mobile dispensaries, 28 family planning centers, 67 leprosy clinics, 28 homes for abandoned children and 32 homes for dying destitutes. They estimated that over a million and a half patients were treated by the mobile dispensaries, and 2,000 were treated with dignity while they were in the process of dying in the homes for the dying, with over 43,000 lepers treated, and they cared for 2,000 abandoned children. They also fed millions of starving people.

Jawaharlal Nehru, the first Prime Minister when India won its independence, inaugurated Mother Teresa's children's home in New Delhi. His daughter was Indira Gandhi, a great friend of hers. Indira served as the third Prime Minister of India from 1966 to 1977 and she was the first female to hold that position. She was the second female head of government in the world and remains the second longest serving female Prime Minister as of 2012.

Two of Mother Teresa's assistants were present at another remarkable incident in which Bali considered another miracle, which Doig also mentioned in his book *Mother Teresa: Her People and Her Work*. This is best presented in Bali's own words: "We were on the street by the governor's house, where the governor used to live. I don't know what the street called there. The other side of the park was where the governor resided and there was big park with a big statue of Queen Victoria.

"I was with Mother Teresa, and there was lots of hustle and bustle. We were having lunch on the sidewalk in Calcutta. All of sudden people began shouting and it became like a roar. I looked at the street and I said, 'What happening?'

"She said, 'It must be some kind of protest going on.' Always Calcutta had some kind of protest so I keep looking at the crowd, and I see this big bull come charging like in a coyote and road runner cartoon. All of a sudden, I warned Mother Teresa, as the bull was coming right to us, 'Look, look, look!'

"And she looked and she said, 'Oh, my God!' She got up right away, and the bull was a few yards from her when she raised her right hand and she shouted very loud, 'Stop!' The bull stopped. He was running so fast, the Brahma bull, very huge, and stopped about three or four feet away from the Mother's feet. It was like a road runner stopping with brakes, with his two front legs stretched out and the other legs were standing, as he stopped. She talked to him and his legs were still stretched while she was talking. I thought he was going to bump her and put her on the 3rd floor of the building next to us because his head was down. I was scared for her.

Sketch by Doig of Chitpur Road, Calcutta

"She scolded the bull by saying, 'You should be ashamed of yourself. Why are you making all this traffic jam and making people so scared?' She was talking to him like a grown up guy. And she said, 'For God's sake, you are causing a traffic jam. You are playing on the street and it is not very fair. You should be ashamed of yourself.' And the bull slowly put one leg up and the other leg up and looked at Mother for a second and turned his head to the other side of the street and went back on the sidewalk, walking back the way he came.

"The people parted and then the traffic started and then all of a sudden everybody say, 'Long live Mother Teresa. Long live Mother Teresa.' It was very dynamic, the ability she had, that much power of the spirit in her. This bull could easily have picked her up and she could have gone to the third floor, easily. She was about 50 or 60 pounds, very tiny, skinny white woman. Short. It would be like a tumbleweed for him, and if he picked his head up and threw her, she would have gone like a ball. Like a tumbleweed. That's what happened. That day everybody was clapping and praising Mother Teresa. That was one miracle I witnessed," Bali concluded.

Doig indicated in his book that a man was knocked down and gored and that nothing could stop the fury of the animal until this reverent Mother stood up to the raging bull.

Mythology in Motion

"Bali, when you dance are you telling a story or are you dancing with the rhythm of the music?" I asked him.

"Dance is part culture and part religion. It's like Catholicism, the bible story. We have our own holy book called *Bhagwat Geeta.*" This is considered the holy epic of Hinduism. "It is very thick and all the saints and sages at that time were full of magic. It was written in Sanskrit but it is translated in many languages. We perform every year as the season turn." Since there are 75 dialogues in India, the spelling of the holy book and its characters may be spelled differently depending on the origin of the translation.

Rama (or Ram in North India) is referred to within Hinduism as Lord of Self-Control or Lord of Virtue: The Perfect Man. Rama is the husband of Sita, whom Hindus consider to be the embodiment of perfect womanhood. Rama's life and journey is one of perfect adherence to *dharma* despite harsh tests of life and time. He is pictured as the ideal man and the perfect human.

I found many tales about Rama. Bali told me his version of one of the legends. "Rama and Lakshmana, two brothers, go to the forest. The demon Ravana came and he found out that Rama's wife Sita was very, very beautiful and he could change himself into an old man. He had the power. So he changed into a small, old man and tried to beg. She was offering him some food, and he said, 'Oh no no no. You have to come near me and give it to me,' and she said no. Before Rama left he put a protective circle around her and warned her, 'You cannot go beyond the circle otherwise you burn to death and no one can step into it.'

"She promised her husband to stay within the circle.

"Ravana said, 'Oh, I can see. This is the curse. I can put my shoes over it and you can put your foot on the shoe. You will not burn.' And he did that and she tried to come out and give food to him and he grabbed her hand and put it on the chariot and left, flying off to Sri Lanka with Sita.

"There were two swans flying nearby and they saw Sita fighting with the old man who became real demon. Sita was terrified and fighting him and so her necklace broke and fell on the ground. One of the swans came back and picked up the necklace. When Rama came back to his house, the swan came and dropped it, and he looked at the swan, picked it up, and he said, 'This belongs to my wife.'

"Then the swan left, then the Hanuman, the Monkey God, appeared and he became a very good friend. He was powerful and huge, like a bear, like Smokey the Bear. Big. He knew how to fly and Rama and Lakshmana don't know where to go but the bird told them which way they were going so he took them by their shoulders, this monkey god, and flew." On this day Rama killed the great demon Ravana, who had abducted Rama's wife Sita to his kingdom of Sri Lanka. Rama, his brother Lakshmana, the Monkey God Hanuman, and an army of monkeys fought a great battle to rescue Sita." The entire narrative is recorded in the epic Ramayana, a Hindu scripture. Several texts also present Hanuman as an incarnation of the Lord Shiva.

Bali concluded, "It's all in the dancing. It is Hindu religion."

The only time and place that Bali attended an annual festival called *Dussehra*, which is a ten day ceremony to honor triumph of Lord Rama over the demon Ravana, was in Old Delhi when he was a teenager. In India effigies of Ravana are constructed all over the city, some standing 60 feet high. They are filled with fireworks. The statues represent the victory of Rama over Ravana, good over evil. It is the biggest festival in India with carnival rides and sweet treats offered. The effigies are set on fire illuminating the statues, then fireworks explode and destroy Ravana. This Burning Man festival is also celebrated throughout India, Nepal, Thailand, Burma and anywhere that there is a large population of Hindus. It is also replicated annually in a week-long art event in the Black Rock Desert in Nevada.

Bali said it was chaos in India every year with tens of thousands of people in streets so crowded it was difficult to walk. There was no traffic allowed and the crowds were so thick when he attended that even strangers had to hold hands, for if they fell they would be trampled to death. He said he remembers it stunk from body odor and urine. The mass of bodies terrified him. One night of the festival was *Ramlila*, which is the story of Rama and Sita re-enacted on a very high stage so that all the people would be able to see the actors. "It is like acting out a bible story."

On the night they burned the effigies, he climbed high into a tree and rested in the branches and watched as the thunderous explosion of fireworks all over the city were set off, creating a suffocating fog of sulfur. Trees were vibrant and beautiful from hundreds of people who climbed on the branches with their red, yellow, blue, green, and various colorful clothing. The demon had ten heads which exploded in all directions after blazing arrows were fired into the statue on the *Ramlila Ground,* in the heart of Old Delhi. Bali stayed in the tree for about three hours after the fireworks until the throngs of people had dwindled.

He told me, "Get your life in order before going to Festival. You are uplifted if you survive." Bali never went back. "I held on to tree branches until after crowd clear. If not, all you see is Bali's bones."

"That's the story. That is what I perform from time to time. Some of the dance romance, some of the dance poetry, and some the real story. Hindu mythology. This is what I do."

"Did the dance troupe that you were with keep the same people or did they change when you went to different places?"

"No, the same group. We cannot change it because other people don't know how the dance goes or what to do, or when to stop, or when not to stop. Different location. Same musicians, same dancers and singers."

"What was the name of your dance troupe?"

"Bali Ram and Dance Company."

The Prince & King of Sikkim

When Bali danced for Mother Teresa in Calcutta, there was a princess from Gengtok, the capital and largest city in Sikkim, in the audience. Doig knew the royal family very well because he had written an article about their small kingdom. The princess approached Doig and said, "We want Bali Ram to come to our country and dance for our father there. It would be nice to have him entertain in our palace. Of course, you are also invited and any of Bali Ram's performers that he needs."

Doig took Bali aside, and said, "The princess of Sikkim wants you to go to Gengtok and perform in the palace."

Bali replied, "Well, if they pay for it, I'll go for it."

Sikkim, independent at that time, is a small kingdom, and the city of Gengtok is located between India and Tibet on the border. With around 600,000 inhabitants, Sikkim is the least populous state in India and the second-smallest state covering approximately 2,740 square miles. Sikkim is the only state in India with an ethnic Nepalese majority, and has eleven official languages.

At that time the king, Tashi Namgyal, was a semi-invalid and not able to travel, so Bali traveled to the king and danced for him. In the audience was the king's son, the *Maharaj Kumar* (prince), whose name was Palden Thondup Namgyal, along with his two small sons, the Prime Minister, and many dignitaries. The prince, the king and the prime minister were in the front row. Most likely the prince's daughter was in the audience also. The ailing king was wrapped in a red robe with a high collar, wearing black loafers and a shiny Sherpa-style hat above his tinted glasses. He had white hair, was very thin and was several inches shorter than Bali, who stood 5'6".

The character of the prince was described by Hope Cooke in her book *Time Change: an Autobiography* as "…his rueful, droll manner, his obvious integrity, and his extraordinary, handsome looks: intelligent dark eyes, smooth bronze skin, sloping cheekbones, and sensual mouth," are what attracted her to him. Cooke and the prince eventually married.

In the photos with Bali, the price appears tall. His back is straight and his head is proud as he holds his sons' hands. He was devastated at the loss of his beloved wife in 1957, Sangey Deki, daughter of a Tibetan dignitary, who gave him three children: *Tenzing, Wangchuk* and *Yangchen*.

Bali stayed overnight at the palace. The next day the king asked Bali, "I very much enjoyed your beautiful dance and you have made my heart very joyful. What would you like to have, Bali Ram? I am very happy to grant you that."

Bali told me, "So I was so stupid. I grew up in Manhattan and India most of the time. I told His Majesty that I like to see the snow. Desmond was there with me and he was clenching his teeth."

2nd from left, Bali Ram, the King, the Prime
Minister, the Prince & his two sons in Gengtok, Sikkim
Photo by Desmond Doig

"Okay, tomorrow morning you can go. The prime minister will take you there," the king told Bali.

When the king left, Doig was furious with Bali. "What the hell, Bali! You could have asked for anything: house, land, whatever you want in life he could have given to you. "

"I don't know. Why didn't you brief me before?"

"So," Bali told me, "that was that. The king had ordered a basket of food to be packed. We had a picnic at the border and I saw the snow. We came back and Desmond was still very, very upset."

He said, "Bali, you're very naïve."

Bali was very young at that time, 18 or 19 years old. "I don't know what to ask king."

I commented to Bali, "It sounds to me as if it was a great gift in your life."

"It *was* a great gift in my life! I danced for this king in the palace. I have some pictures of the king, some photographs with him. I also have a book about him and the prince who became the last *chogyal* (king) of Sikkim.

"After the king died, India took over the kingdom because China was on the border of Sikkim. You can just walk in, walk out. India took it over and India divided the border. There's a lot of army over there now. India made a base in the kingdom. So it belongs to India now."

The prince was young when Bali danced for him and his father, and Bali said, "It like a fairy tale. I had so much opportunity, but I was very naïve. I tried to be just me, that's all. From childhood, I am not greedy at all. I am very fair, very practical. I don't have a greedy mind. I don't care about things, I just need to live, although I don't care about luxury, it comes to me whatever it is. I enjoy life."

Sikkim is a landlocked Indian state nestled in the Himalayan Mountains. The state borders Nepal to the west, China's Tibet Autonomous Region to the north and east, and Bhutan to the southeast, while the state of West Bengal lies to the south. Cooke described Gangtok as, "When you cross the border from India, it's a different world – electricity, neat houses, clean bazaars….All the government buildings, schools, chest clinic, cottage industries, hospital, printing press, secretariat, etc….are built in traditional Sikkimses curved-roof architecture. All have bright blue roofs, Maharaj Kumar (the prince) feeling it worth a little extra money to give people a cheerful, cohesive environment…Gangtok gives the impression of being a model town in a social studies book."

Kangchenjunga, the world's third-highest peak, is located on Sikkim's border with Nepal. Sikkim is a popular tourist destination, owing to its culture, scenery and biodiversity. It also has the only open border between India and China.

Gengtok in the territory of Sikkim

A Home in New Delhi

When I questioned him about what he did with his earnings, Bali said, "I take some of the money and go to Kashmir (also known as Cashmere) where India was fighting Pakistan over the territories." India and Pakistan were still fighting over Kashmir at the United Nations in 2010. Pakistan and India both claim that Kashmir belongs to them. Kashmir is a region in South-central Asia. The term Kashmir historically was described as the valley just to the south of the western end of the Himalayan mountain range. Today, Kashmir refers to a much larger area. People like it for its natural beauty and simple lifestyle.

Bali would rent a houseboat in Kashmir. One day he was going to the market and a very tall, handsome guy came by on a motorcycle. He came into the shop and asked Bali, "Is this guy bothering you?" referring to the shopkeeper.

Bali said, "No no. We just talking."

He introduced himself as the chief of police, and gave his name, obviously having a little fun with the proprietor.

"How very nice. My name is Bali Ram."

"I know who you are because we read about you."

Bali said, "It has been very nice to meet you, but I'm leaving now."

"I'm leaving, too. I can drop you off at your houseboat?"

"Certainly. I do not drive." Bali had never learned to drive.

When they reached the boathouse, the chief said, "Do you mind if I visit you?"

"No, of course not. Bring your friends, too." The chief of police brought the mayor and others of his entourage and they had a wonderful time during the month that Bali rented the houseboat, which was annually during the summertime. They developed a great friendship and he met many Kashmiri people. Bali avoided his parents' home in Nepal because of his disgruntled and disappointed father.

With his earnings, he built his own house in New Delhi, the capital of India. Hope Cooke described the capital territory of Delhi as, "Not only is it the most beautiful place I've ever been, but I can love it for its soul as well. Here's a place, unlike the Middle East, with a conscience. Also, very important, here people have not become so westernized that they've cut off their history. They're in touch with their past, drawing strength from it. There's less gap between rich and poor, and there's a chance to work in community development that will uplift the whole country, not just the elite or the cities...Pony-drawn *tongas* clip by."

His house was like a palace to him and it was very large with beautiful bedrooms. His caretaker was a very wonderful woman, a widow, who had four children. Bali was doing world tours at the time and when he finished each tour, he went to his house in India. He put her completely in charge. She could cook whatever she wanted. She could invite anybody she wanted. Her children, all boys, grew up in the house. Whenever Bali came home they all sat down and ate together just like a family. "She's the boss, she portions everybody's plate. She's like a mother to me because my mother was in Nepal and she could not come."

His father would not stop his drinking. Finally Shanti, his mother, got so disgusted with him that she left her husband in Nepal and moved to her son's house in New Delhi, living with his servants after Bali relocated to America. His father became very ill and had about a month to live when he showed up at Bali's house. Still a devoted Nepalese wife, Shanti started caring for him as he was dying. He had to quit drinking, he had no other choice. Medicine was no longer effective because his liver was destroyed from drinking. He was bed ridden and she cleaned him, bathed him, and fed him.

"She did that because she was a Nepalese woman. And then he died," Bali said. "He was calling my name before he died."

Shanti began shouting at her husband saying, "It's too late. It's too late. Your son is not going to listen. He's not here."

She lived about a month after that, and then she also died. Bali said they had been together since they were children. "It was not unusual that husband and wife die same day in the same bed because of their lifetime bond," Bali told me.

When he began living mostly in America, Bali tried to sign over his property and the house to his housekeeper. In India he went to court to make it official. The judge said, "You cannot do that."

Bali asked, "Why?"

The judge responded, "You have to sell it. You cannot just give it away."

"Why can't I give my house as a gift?"

"Such a large gift, you can't do that."

"Okay." Bali said. "If I must sell it, I will."

So Bali put his hand in his pocket and it was empty. He asked Bill Haines, his manager, if he had any cash. Haines had two Indian rupees in paper money, which is about ten cents, so he walked over to Bali to hand it to him, but Bali ordered, "Give it to her."

Bali asked his housekeeper, "Do you have any money?"

Looking at the money in her hand, she said, "Yes."

Bali asked her, "How much money you have?"

"Two rupees."

Bali said pointing to the signature line, "Sign this paper here. My house is sold to you for two rupees."

She handed the two rupees back to Bali to seal the deal. The judge was furious because the judge had thought he could get some share of the sale. Bali said that at that time, with Indian judges and lawyers, one could pay them off and nothing would happen. "Very bad custom," Bali said shaking his head.

"Do you still go back to the house?" I asked.

"Yeah, I can go back and stay there. It's her house, actually. I'm the big brother kind of thing. Her children got married and their children living in that house now. I'm very happy I did that. I have no brother, no sister. My mom and dad died. I never got to the funeral of my father because he was very mean to me. I never received his blessing or anything. But I did, in my way, have a very, very hard life. A very hard life, but I came through and now I'm here."

An Evening with Picasso

While performing in Paris with Indrani, a man that Bali described as not very tall, just an average man, came up to Bali after the show and said, "My name is Pablo Picasso."

Bali responded, "Oh, how nice," describing himself as "not knowing beans about him."

Picasso moved into the crowd for a moment, giving Bali and Indrani's manager, an American, a chance to explain the significance of the man who had just introduced himself. "Bali, he's Pablo Picasso!"

"What is he? Who is he?"

"He's a very famous painter."

"Oh, I am very sorry. I don't know about him."

Picasso came back with a smile on his face and asked Bali, "How long are you staying in France?"

"Oh, just two days. We have engagements in other countries."

"Two day, huh? Well then, there is no time to spare. Come with me tomorrow. I would like to take you to a village, and I will introduce you to the dance of my country. Will you come with me?"

"Ah, yes."

Tom, Indrani's manager said, "I will have to come with you."

"Can our manager come with me?" Bali asked Picasso.

"Yes, of course."

"I will have a car pick you and take you to the Paris airport."

Bali was part of Indrani's troupe while touring Europe. Bali said that Indrani didn't go because it was very late at night and she was afraid to go. Tom went with Bali because he didn't know where Picasso was taking him. He thought he was throwing a party for them.

They boarded a small plane. Picasso brought two other friends with him. Bali thought the plane landed in Italy, most likely it was southern France. They would not have gone to Spain since Picasso was in a self-exile from Spain after 1936 and never returned. Born and raised in Spain, Picasso lived in Paris and in southern France. He was overtly political before and after World War II. Besides his renowned paintings - creating something artistic every day - he also wrote poetry, and was a sculpture, printmaker, ceramicist, and a stage designer. Picasso also played himself in a few films. An international celebrity, Picasso was considered the most influential living artist of the 20th century. Bali was as dedicated to his dance as Picasso to his painting, and, therefore, they were very similar in their devotion to their art.

Picasso took them from the landing field in a jeep, and they drove until they arrived at a small village which Bali never knew its' name. It was evening and there was one bulb hanging from the tree in the empty town square. Bali was amazed how quickly the news of Picasso's arrival spread. It was a place that the artist (a womanizer) loved to visit. All of a sudden people came: two people, four people, eight people, a dozen people, and before Bali knew it, about 50 people were gathered in the square. It was party time.

One small table was placed under the tree. Out of the crowd came beautiful women who were dancers. Bali described his experience. "It was so fascinating to me because I saw in the films, but not real in life, *flamenco* dancers. "

The Spanish word *flamenco* literally means flamingo, resembling the form of the elegant bird which is not only native to Southern Spain but can be found all along the migratory routes of the Romani people across North Africa even to their origin in India. The dance style of *flamenco* may well have originated in or strongly influenced by the expressive dance of northwestern India.

There were four or five dancers, taking their turns on the top of the table while the music played and the musicians sang. The clicking of the castanets was in rhythm to the tapping of their feet.

The entire time, Picasso was sketching and painting the women while they were dancing, soaking up how they were standing, watching and sketching all their movements and gestures. Bali said there were many plump women in the village and he thought Picasso was sketching them, also. Many times during my conversations with Bali, he referred back to that magical night, and how mesmerized he was, and how indelible his memory was of the *flamenco* dancers with their raven hair flying in the air while they twirled and stomped on the table top in the moonlight. Men and women danced. Sometimes two men. Sometimes a man and a woman.

In the book, *Pablo Picasso His life and Times, a Biography* by Pierre Cabanne, during Picasso's picador era of paintings, the author described the picador. "The girls display their luscious breasts for him, wiggle their rumps, dance nude to the accompaniment of castanets, and he applauds without ever becoming aroused…..So Picasso surrounds him (the picador) with a ballet of deadly winks, globular bosoms with brown nipples, hairy armpits, rounded belies, appetizing hips, skirts, mantillas, obscene gestures. Sweat makes the girls' long black hair stick to their temples as they dance in the musky odor of their bodies. Castanets click, the guitar accompanies the wild gyrations of the women, urged on with clapping of hands and beating of feet."

Bali says of his experience, "The women were magnificent, beautiful hair below the butt, black and skinny, skinny like a twig. Beautiful. Beautiful. Dancing on this table. I forgot about Picasso and everybody. I was just looking at these people. It was incredibly beautiful. The footwork was just like Indian dancing but different style. I was beguiled. It was outside in the village under a tree in 1964. Just one tree. A big square. One bulb hanging off a branch and they brought a small table about this big (he gestured with his arms to indicate about 40" in diameter) and these people got on the table. Someone played an accordion and they started dancing. It was fascinating! It was mesmerizing. It was so beautiful."

He returned to Paris the same night with Picasso, arriving early in the morning. Picasso loved many forms of artwork. Bali said it was an honor to meet Picasso, and to have the experience of that magic night. "So, I had a night with Picasso."

The Emperor of Ethiopia

Bali was in New York dancing at the United Nations, a man came to him and asked if Bali would dance for his king, explaining that he was Berhanu Dinke, the ambassador of Ethiopia. Bali said, "Forgive me, your Excellency. Who is your king?"

The Dinke told Bali the ruler's name was Haile Selassie and he was considered an emperor. Indrani was invited by Nehru to dance for Selassie in 1956 in Delhi, India, before she began touring with Bali.

"I am sorry, your Excellency. I would like to dance for him but I do not have transportation."

"We just want to know whether you can or cannot. We will provide you with all the transportation." He took Bali's phone number. Two days later he called Bali and said, "One week from now we'll send a limousine to your apartment."

When the limousine came it was long, sleek, and black. All of his neighbors in his four story apartment came out to gawk and said, "What the heck? Where'd you get this one," and, "Where are you going?"

"I don't know," he replied. "I'm not going anywhere." But he was on his way to the airport. The emperor sent his own plane to take Bali to Ethiopia. Bali and his manager stepped into the plane. Bali was amazed at the splendor and opulence. Blue carpet lined the floors and everything was trimmed in gold: the chair, sofa, picture frames, the lamp, and all the lights in the plane. He said it was like flying in a luxurious living room. It was very beautiful. Lots of ivory and gold. The arms of the chairs were ivory with gold caps and gold leaves. He and his manager looked at each other astonished, and his manager said, "You've got class, Bali Ram."

They arrived in Ethiopia and were escorted to the palace. The emperor came out to greet Bali with two leopards beside him on leashes. Bali froze. He was afraid that the large cats might attack him.

"Your majesty, I am very scared of your leopards."

"Okay, Bali, but they don't bite," Emperor Haile Selassie told him.

"I know they are very friendly, but please...." Wearing a golden turban, Haile Selassie handed the leashes to his entourage, and led them to his palace.

The Jubilee Palace was completed in 1955, a modern palace built to mark Emperor Haile Selassie's Silver Jubilee. This large cream-colored Palace had three grand pillared porticos on its front that rose the height of the building. The Emperor moved into the palace and made it his primary residence, which had stately grounds, impressive fountains and an interesting collection of animals in its zoo, as witnessed by Bali firsthand. The gates of the Palace were topped by large carved lions. The Emperor lived here between 1961 and 1974.

Bali performed twice: once in the palace and once outdoors. In his presence, Bali said he didn't know if he was on earth or cloud nine. Bali was told that Haile Selassie was a direct descendant of Adam and Eve. Bali replied with astonishment, "I didn't know Adam and Eve were black!"

Bali stayed four days and saw many beautiful sites, the names of which he couldn't recall. He did remember that they ate a lot of watermelon. He said watermelon was everywhere.

The first night Bali danced for the emperor and the second night, after Bali's performance, Haile Selassie danced for him. He danced so gracefully and so beautifully in the evening light. When he was turning, Bali saw the perspiration on his body, and his body appeared to be blue in the moonlight. He was wearing a short white wrap with a gold belt and jewels were swaying around his neck. The performances were packed with people. When Bali danced outdoors, he said that he was overwhelmed with people surrounding him and trying to shake hands with him.

The Jubilee Palace was the site of the dethronement of Emperor Haile Selassie in 1974, when he was officially removed by a group of low ranking officers. They renamed the palace the "National Palace" and the current government of Ethiopia continues to refer to it by that name.

Sir Edmund Hillary's Expedition

Breakfast was being served as Doig and Bali sat at the table sipping tea. A knock on the front door interrupted their leisure.

"Excuse me, Bali. I believe we have early morning company." Doig's servant came into the breakfast room and announced that Sir Edmund Hillary and his Nepalese Sherpa, Tenzing Norgay, were asking to be admitted.

"Of course. Show them in," Doig said. "Ed, Norgay, so good to see you," and he offered them breakfast or tea. "Please, have a seat. What brings you out at this time of the day?"

Hillary came to this highly respected reporter to announce his intention of forming a Himalayan scientific and mountaineering expedition that would be several months long beginning in 1960. Not only was he giving Doig the scoop, but he also asked him to be their correspondent accompanying the adventurers. Doig was an expert linguist who loved the Sherpa people, and along with his writing skills, this made him Hillary's first choice. The beginning and the end of the story involves Bali. Once again this shows the times that Bali was witness to extraordinary events, and that he met some of the world's most prominent and interesting people. Does this chapter belong in Bali's story? Maybe not, but I found a wealth of information in Doig's book *High in the Thin Cold Air* and I think my readers will understand the link to Bali and enjoy Doig's adventure.

Tenzing was considered the most famous mountain climber in history as he was one of the first two individuals known to have reached the summit of Mount Everest, which he accomplished with Edmund Hillary in1953, on an earlier expedition.

Norgay Tensing

One might think of Sherpas as guides in the Himalayas. Doig described them as such. "There are eighteen distinct Sherpa tribes, each with their own traditions and taboos, many speaking dialects of their own. The Sherpa language is very similar to Tibetan and employs the Tibetan script so that Tibetans and Sherpas have no difficulty in understanding each other. Men and women dress in the Tibetan style." They were Mongolians originally from eastern Tibet. *Shar* means east and *pa* means people so they were people from the east centuries ago.

Hillary had two objectives. The first part of the expedition was to establish or disprove the existence of Yetis, which are commonly referred to as Abominable Snowmen, Sasquatch, or Bigfoot. Hillary had the lofty ambition of capturing a live specimen. *Capchur* guns (probably phoenic for "capture") were taken on the expedition, which were powerful air rifles that would anesthetize large animals and allow the men to capture, examine, and treat animals medically if needed. Self-operating tripwire cameras were also included in the event a Yeti could not be captured; they would produce a photograph of the animal. The second objective of the expedition was to compile high altitude physiological research to test the effectiveness of long acclimatization. Some of the peaks rose to a breathtaking height of 27,790 feet.

Thirty tons of expedition supplies and equipment had to be carried on foot by 500 porters. The supplies were mostly carried on the backs of the local Sherpa tribe members, each assigned sixty pounds. In fact, women were also used, stacking a child on top of their load. Each member of the expedition had to pack and carry his personal items.

Dawa Tensing was the *sirdar* or foreman and had been on every mountaineering expedition since 1952. Considered an old school Sherpa, he had plaited hair. His team had lined up in the hotel tennis court. Doig described the lot as wearing "scarlet Japanese silk, saffron cotton, turquoise blue English nylon, multi-colored wool. Gold pendant earrings and occasional plaits of well-greased hair look incongruous among heavily padded jackets, woolen trousers, and boots. There are even a few striped pajama suits that are startling. And necklaces. But the smiles are uniform, spontaneous, infectious."

In 1958 tragedy struck Dawa Tensing while he and his son were on separate expeditions. His wife got word they were both killed in an avalanche. Stricken with grief his wife threw herself into a river and drowned. When Tensing returned home he had to face a double tragedy, for not only had his wife died, but indeed, his son had been killed in the avalanche.

Hillary knew it was necessary that what he referred to as "arty types" of people, were included, along with the serious mountaineers. Among those, were Desmond Doig and Marlin Perkins who, at the time, was the director of the Lincoln Park Zoo in Chicago and also a TV personality. Marlin was the host of the TV show *Wild Kingdom*.

One of the sponsors was the *World Book Encyclopedia*. Their representative, John Dienhart, had shopped in New York for his "kit." Doig described it saying, "His personal kit could equip a small expedition, and it looks as colorful as a Fifth Avenue shop window. He has pep pills and tranquilizers, foot freezers and foot warmers, dental floss and perfumed face cleaner, tissues, ointments, aid for the fainthearted, Bermuda shorts, the lot."

Doig commented about the packing and sorting their personal items: "The uninitiated, sort out our own difficult affairs – whether to sacrifice foot sprays and bath salts for cans of beer, and custom-built boots for the expedition clodhoppers, for example, or take the lot and die under the load. Does one ever know what a load is like until one is under it and has walked with it a mile, five miles, eight, or fifteen? Does one suspect that elegant hiking shorts bought with a wife or girlfriend in a moment of distant and deep-freeze heroism are not quite designed with an Eastern sun and Nepalese leeches in mind?" He was unprepared for the amount of walking that was required each day and the weight of his rucksack, but managed, with humor and British perseverance, to keep up with the group.

"No other day was quite like that memorable first," Doig penned. "We grew blisters and we got bored. We let the stubble develop on our chins and became blasé about our appearances. Even though we subconsciously resisted it – cursing the sun, the rain, the ups the downs – we fell for the magic of Nepal, on the second, and third, and the umpteenth day. The vastness: looking suddenly for miles through windows in the mist. The silence: hearing a jackal cry on another mountain and in the night waking to feel the vibration of the stars. And beauty: of terraced fields on the limbs of mountains, trees wearing orchids, flowers, and prayer flags beside cairns of stones...On and on through forest and across bare wind-swept ridges, through lush rice fields and surprised villages, across torrents spanned by a single log and across rivers on chain bridges fashioned by local blacksmiths and chance. We toiled up slopes we normally would ignore, lungs bursting and souls despairing, and down slopes we normally would leave to avalanches and the insane. Always there was beauty to take our flagging minds off the weary business of endlessly walking, and the pains and frustrations of endlessly walking to take our minds off the beauty of our surroundings."

Days began early and luxuries such as tea in bed, newspapers, chilled beer, dry martinis, hot toddies, feather beds, steaming cups of hot chocolate, a leisurely warm bath, and clean clothes were gone. Their baths and meals were communal. "I wait for the day when a Sherpa turns his camera on a wallowing of naked sahibs and a Sherpa anthropologist tries to explain the phenomenon," Doig commented.

There were sightings of Yeti tracks by previous European mountaineers, but the Sherpas claimed sightings, hearing their strange whistling, finding footprints in the snow, and even a scalp that would require patient negotiations to be turned over for scientific examination. The Sherpas from the villages of Solu Khumbu and Langtang both gave descriptions of three varieties of Yetis. These ranged from up to twenty feet tall to a wizened, manlike creature the size of young man. At 18,000 feet they found their first footprints. Doig said he almost killed himself scaling the three miles to see the footprints. He took a plaster cast of one footprint which measured eleven inches in length by five inches wide. Due to crude conditions while drying out the cast, it is forever fused to a slab of stone.

There were four mail runners who left the camps at about 18,000 feet in altitude going to Kathmandu and back, a trip which took seven to eight days covering a distance of 120 to 170 miles depending on the camp site. Doig said, "They ran light, in pairs for company and protection, without the comfort of a tent or bedding. They carried meager rations to see them over the uninhabited reaches of the track and otherwise ate in the villages in which they rested."

One of the runners, Lakhpa, told Doig, "We were almost carried away by the wind. It screamed at us all the while; our faces froze, and we thought we would die. Fortunately Rin Norbu (his companion) remembered the right prayers." They were tough characters.

The "Silver Hut" was constructed at their camp at 19,000 feet for supplies and equipment, as sleeping and cooking quarters, and, of course, for shelter. They also built what they referred to as the "Green Hut." Both were framed from local timber, wire netting, and a layer of tar paper, with a final layer of canvas. They housed a stove for heat and cooking and held up very adequately for the sub zero temperatures and ferocious winds. Other camps at lower elevations were dismantled when the expedition ended.

The typical Sherpa house was described by Doig as "a solid affair; two storied, white rough-cast walls, gabled roofs tiled with shingles or covered with logs, and floors of rammed earth and wood. More often than not they are semi-detached, the two or three sections unconnected and occupied by related families.

"On the cavernous, windowless ground floor are rooms for the cattle, farm implements, firewood, and fodder. Negotiating these obstacles (and one has to) as through them is access to the stairs and the upper floor, is something of a nightmare. Animals snuffle and move in the dark; one may stumble over a sleeping yak or onto the sharp horns of a Tibetan sheep."

Khumjung is a village that most of the Sherpas came from and it was the home of the legendary Yeti scalp. The scalp was kept in a box and three village elders had to be present when it was exposed. Hillary, Doig and Perkins were presented with the scalp to be placed on their heads in turn. Doig described it as, "a mystifying object, dome-shaped and sparsely covered with black and henna bristles, obviously of some age, and to all appearances the scalp of a powerful anthropoid — most likely contender the mountain gorilla. From sawn-off base to pointed crown it was eight inches deep, seven inches in width, and ten inches long at its oval base." He said it was remarkably well preserved considering it was claimed to be at least 200 years old.

The elders claimed it was genuine Yeti and that the valleys around their village were heavily populated with the man-like creatures which seemed to be all well and good until they began to eat villagers. The legend goes as such:

One day, two hundred and more years ago, when a man, his son, and daughter had been slain and eaten by a Yeti, the people of the Sherpa valleys decided the Yetis must be liquidated. But how? The Yetis were powerful creatures; they were in a distinct majority and had acquired a taste for human blood. A certain learned lama, Rolwa Dorji by name, formulated a somewhat irreligious plan, considering lamas must never take life. Large vats of chang (a native beer made from rice) were brought out in full view of the watching Yetis; the villagers pretended to drink their fill and then to fight to the death among themselves. The swords the villagers used for the mock battle were made of wood; at dusk when they stole from the battleground where they had been simulating death all day they took the precaution of leaving genuine, well-sharpened swords behind them and, of course, the chang.

Alas, for Yetis, they were splendid mimics. At nightfall they descended from their rocky fortress where they had occupied a grandstand view of the Sherpa battle, drank the potent chang, and, getting drunk, fought to death. In the morning only one rather dazed Yeti remained. This Lama Rolwa Dorji personally slew and carried its carcass back to his monastery in triumph.

So the scalp ended up in Khumjung where Hillary was bargaining with the elders to borrow it for three months and take it out of the country for scientific examinations. Three months were negotiated down to six weeks which was a very brief time to descend, make travel arrangements, and take the object to America, France and Britain along with a Nepalese representative,

Khunjo Chumbi.   Chumbi was the keeper of village documents, deeds, and ancient books of law and order.

When the group escorting Doig and Hillary arrived at Khumjung, it was party time.   Chumbi was considered the dance champion of Lhasa, in which he performed nonstop for twelve hours.   Doig described blue-eyed Khunjo Chumbi as being the perfect representative of the Sherpa society to accompany him. He said he had strong Mongolian features, plaited hair, turquoise earrings, embroidered felt boots, and a swagger that "agitates" his magenta robes.   "One of the gods was giving trouble," Chumbi told Hillary.

"Which god?"

"Oh, one of the mortal ones," Chumbi said with a wink.

"Could the god's anger be appeased?" Hillary asked.

"Yes, of course, but it would cost 500 rupees."

Cash was scarce on the expedition, and although it amounted to $66, Hillary countered, "Would the god consider a reduction?"

"Absolutely none. His anger was great!" Chumbi held fast.

"Alright. Five hundred rupees we will pay," with the earnest hope that no more gods would suffer fits of bad temper.

On foot from Khumjung to Kathmandu was between a 14 and 17 day trip each way, so they wanted to arrange a helicopter to transport the scalp. Doig and Chumbi would be the caretakers of the scalp for six weeks. An article of agreement with the village elders was drawn up and was signed by Hillary, Perkins, and Doig on November 19, 1960. Three head expedition

Sherpas also signed the document, and then it was party time again.

Of course, Chumbi, a village elder, would be visiting with President Eisenhower, Queen Elizabeth, and the King of Nepal. Protocol dictated that he must bring them typical Nepalese gifts. These included bags of finely ground wheat flour, sacred scroll paintings, bricks of Tibetan tea, and dried yak's tails, and gems. Doig said he was tortured with doubts and prayed that the western world's well defined boundaries "would be kind to this innocently naïve villager from Khumjung." Tibetan tea is traditionally drunk with yak butter and salt. The wheat flour called *tsampa* is a Sherpa staple and an offering of hospitality and friendship. The adorned yak tails are used as fly swatters and were essential in his country to shoo the annoying flies away that were swarming everywhere.

Doig and Chumbi rushed madly to visit America, Paris, and London in the allotted time. Bali Ram was delighted that his dear friend stopped briefly to visit him in New York on his way from Chicago and showed him the scalp.

"Oh, it is so good for you to visit me," Bali told Doig. "How long can you stay?"

"Just a couple of hours. We are off to the airport on a whirlwind tour to have the scalp authenticated by world authorities." They caught up quickly on events in each of their lives and Bali gave his friend a teary-eyed hug, as Doig left Bali's apartment. It meant a great deal to Bali that his friend stopped by for a brief and coveted visit.

The reporter and the Sherpa handed the scalp to scientific researchers to authenticate. The professionals at the Chicago Natural History Museum judged it to be from a blue bear. Professor Millot of the Musee de l'Homme in Paris declared the scalp fake. Chumbi responded, "In Nepal we have neither giraffes nor kangaroos so we know nothing about them. In France there are no Yetis so I sympathize with your ignorance."

London was very gracious to this Nepalese visitor, and he was invited to Buckingham Palace so that he could present his most unusual gifts to Queen Elizabeth who was in Sandringham at the time. Doig and Chumbi were received at the palace by a Royal attendant who said, "Her majesty has commanded me to receive you and thank you and your people for the most generous gift and good wishes. Her Majesty is most touched."

"What about her children?" Chumbi asked.

"The royal children are very well, Mr. Chumbi, thank you."

"Please tell the Queen that I am not too disappointed not meeting her because the Queen and I have many thousands of lives yet to live. In one of them we will certainly meet. And tell the Queen that I think she must be a very great Queen because she has made me very happy today. It is the job of a Queen to make poor people happy."

Doig hoped that his gifts would not offend the Queen.

While in England Doig took Chumbi to his family home in Kent where his mother and father lived and his family had gathered for the holidays. He introduced the Sherpa to his first western Christmas. Chumbi was not prepared to exchange Christmas gifts, so emptied his purse and he gave Doig's mother one of his most prized possessions, a brooch with a photograph of the Dali Lama.

In January 1961, during the time of the expedition, Queen Elizabeth and her husband, the Duke of Edinburgh, made a state visit to Nepal. The gracious queen asked to meet Khunjo Chumbi to thank him personally for her gifts that he presented to her representative in England. He and his 45-year-old, nine month pregnant wife, walked from Khumjung to Kathmandu along with some expedition Sherpas. During the 180 mile journey, Mrs. Chumbi gave birth along the roadside. "I did not want to miss you," she told the Queen at a British Embassy reception, "so I wasted no time about having the child and decided to keep up with the men (who stopped for breakfast). That was only five days ago." They named their fourth son Phillip in honor of the Duke.

Marlin Perkins, Ed Hillary,
Khunj Chumbi, & Desmond Doig

Since the scientists in London thought the Yeti scalp was not authentic either, Chumbi brought a shaggy, henna-colored arm of a Snowman to show the Queen. Doig said that the Queen and Duke examined it and decided without a doubt that it was the hind leg of a blue bear. They did not refute the Sherpa's believe in his presence. In the end, no one could or would confirm the scalp was that of a Yeti, giving other animals the credit for its origin. Of course, the Sherpa knew first hand that the examiners were mistaken through their ignorance.

President John F. Kennedy

Bali had been in New York, had performed in many places including Carnegie Hall, packed his clothes, and returned to India. He received word from the dance academy, which he was associated with for a few years after graduation, that the dean was waiting for him. He went to the dean's office. The man was very excited, and he ushered Bali into his office, holding a piece of paper in his trembling hand. "President Kennedy sent me this letter and he wants you to come to United States and perform."

"No. I don't know. I'm not going."

The dean was shocked. "What? Do you know what you're saying?"

Bali said, "Yeah. I'm not going," and he started walking out. Bali was aware that President Kennedy was inaugurated to serve after President Eisenhower. Bali knew he had no monetary means to make the journey and it would require a large troupe of dancers and musicians.

"You can take anybody, anything from this school. As many people you want, whoever *you* want," shouted the dean.

Bali stopped right there, frozen in his tracks and turned around in disbelief. "Can I?"

"Yes. You may."

"Then I go." Thirty-five people were chosen to accompany Bali to New York to perform at the United Nations.

Bali handed me a photograph and said, "See that picture? It was taken at the United Nations. President Kennedy was there when I performed." Bali didn't know if they would like the Indian dancing, or the music, or the costumes, but they evidently enjoyed it very much. The cropped photograph shows Bali and Indrani performing on stage. In the front row are the backs of President Kennedy and Jackie, with his head tipped towards his wife.

The stage at the United Nations was spacious which gave the performers the room needed to dance and play instruments. Bali said, "These are my people. I picked them to dance with me from my school." Indrani Rahman, who won the Miss India pageant in 1952, accompanied Bali.

Preceding the dance, there is a warm up on stage to get the body ready for the dance. Bali described it as the opening up of a flower. It was just improvised rhythm, with no meaning, just a warm up, and it was an invocation to the gods to give them protection and make them popular with the audience. When he appears on stage, he dances barefoot with five-pound bells attached to each ankle. His chest is bare except for his ornate choker, with bangles on his wrists and arm bands on his upper arms.

Original caption: Brilliant Job by Bali Ram and Indrani
(on stage at the United Nations, U.S.A.)

Bali's adornments, Bend, Oregon, U.S.A.
Photo by Daniel Biggs, Jr.

His dancing garment, *dhoti*, is attached with a large belt. Eyes are made up with black liners and his hair was tied in a type of knot when he had long hair.

The language the singer used was a very classical language Tamiel. "You are improvising with the rhythm," he said. There was not just one way to dance and play, and yet it was all synchronized. Singers and musicians accompanied the dancers and they performed a lot of different dances.

The musicians beat different drums including the *mendrum*, a large drum that rests on the player's right ankle and foot. One musician used the *venu*, which is an Indian flute made of bamboo, and another played the *manjira*, which look like cymbals made of brass. The musicians would perform about two minutes.

There were two singers. Sometimes all of the troupe would perform, sometimes only the drummer, or only a singer, sometimes only the girls, or sometimes Bali was not on stage. Occasionally there was no dancing or singing, only music. They kept it always interesting for the audience. All the performers would come on stage for the finale. A woman handed Bali an armful of flowers. In India, they always practice respect and honor the elders. Bali told me, "I accept it. I give it to the oldest man (in the troupe) out of respect."

While Bali was touring the world, he was the only male dancer of classical Indian dance in the Western hemisphere. Bissano Ram Gopal, born in1917, who preceded Bali Ram as the only male, was an Indian dancer and choreographer who performed mostly as a soloist and toured extensively throughout his lengthy career. A modernist, he blended the classical Indian dance with balletic choreography and was among the first to showcase Indian classical dance in the West starting in the 1930's. Gopal opened two dance schools for a short while, first in Bangalore before moving to England and later The Academy of Indian Dance and Music in London in 1962. In his later years, he lived in London, Venice and the south of France. Gopal was the performer who inspired Shala Mattingly.

At end of the show, the President came back stage to meet him, but couldn't stay long because he had another appointment. That was the first time Bali met Kennedy.

"It was the very highlight of my being as Bali Ram. It was incredible. All these dignitary and people I met I wish I could meet them again. I didn't even have enough sense to value it at that time. My senses were off. I was still very young while in the United States."

A Stroll with Kennedy

In the fall of 1961 Indrani was invited by The Asia Society in New York to tour the United States with her troupe. In *Dancing in the Family*, Sukanya Rahman told about the tour. "She (her mother Indrani) took with her three musicians from Bangalore – a vocalist, Lokiah; a flautist, Srinivasa Murthy; and a drummer, Seshadri. Her dancers included Bali Ram, a darkly handsome, statuesque Bharata Natyam dancer." She named other members of her troupe.

Jawaharlal Nehru, the first Prime Minister of independent India from 1947 until 1964, was visiting the U.S. The high point of the tour was an invitation from Nehru as Rahman described, "To perform at the Indian embassy in Washington, at a special *Diwali* celebration he was hosting for President and Mrs. Kennedy.

"In Nehru's honor, Jacqueline Kennedy wore a dress with a bodice encrusted with red gems to match Nehru's signature red rose in his lapel. The glittering event was attended by Indira Gandhi, President Kennedy, his mother Rose Kennedy, Jacqueline Kennedy's sister, Princess Lee Radziwell, her mother and stepfather, Mr. and Mrs. Hugh Achincloss, and Ambassador B. K. Nehru and his wife.

"A small makeshift stage, with a tiny screen to serve as a greenroom, had been set up for the dancers. What the audience witnessed was a dazzling performance of three styles of dance – Bharata Natyam, Kuchipudi, and Odissi.

"What the audience didn't see was all the mayhem behind the screen as the four dancers tried to make elaborate costume changes."

Bali told me, "I was all shook up," to meet the President again.

Kennedy took Bali aside and said that he would like Bali to meet his family at the Kennedy estate in Florida.

"Oh, I would be honored to meet your family."

Arrangements were made and Bali flew to Palm Beach which was referred to as the Winter White House, located 65 miles north of Miami, along millionaire's row, to meet his mom and dad "and all the mini Kennedys" as Bali described two-year-old John-John, five-year-old Caroline, and many of their cousins.

"So I met Joseph Kennedy (the patriarch, confined to a wheel chair and unable to speak after a stroke), Ted, and Bobby Kennedy." Bobby Kennedy was serving as a state senator in New York at that time.

Kennedy's Palm Beach House

"Where we going?" Bali asked Kennedy, as they left the house after lunch and he beckoned Bali to follow.

"We're going for a walk on the beach," he answered dressed in a T-shirt and blue jeans, kicking his tennis shoes off to go barefoot on the beach.

Bali told me, "He looked just like any other American and his hair had lots of red highlights in the Florida sunshine."

As they began their stroll together, three helicopters hovered overhead but they were far enough away that they could talk in private without the whir of the engine interfering.

The President seemed seven foot tall to Bali's 5'6, and he said that Kennedy, who was actually 6'1, stooped to talk with him as he asked him about his dancing and his life. Bali told him he was also going to school at Columbia in New York.

Kennedy asked Bali how long he had been performing: Did he plan to stay in America? Did he have a lover? Was Indrani married and how long had they danced together? According to her book, Sukanya Rahman said, "Gossip circulated that John F. Kennedy had tried, through embassy officials, to set up a date with my mother — she never confirmed or denied these rumors. The next day (after the performance at the Embassy) the newspapers in the U.S. and in India were filled with pictures of my mother smiling up at the handsome, young American president."

Bali said that all of the President's questions were respectful and had not indicated that Kennedy asked him to approach Indrani or set him up with her.

"Where will you be going for your next performance?"

"I am going to L.A."

The President said, "Oh, wonderful. Somebody will come to see you."

"Who?"

"Never mind, you'll see." They returned to the house after their fifteen minute stroll and Bali returned to his apartment in New York the same day.

Tea with Marilyn

Los Angeles. When Bali finished his dance, he went to the green room which was his dressing room to take off his makeup. A man assigned to Bali by the performance hall was assisting him. Bali couldn't remember the name of the performance hall, but he said it was a very large, professional theater, three stories high. There was a knock on the door and the assistant opened it and somebody handed him a card. "Oh my God, Bali! It says Marilyn Monroe," and Bali looked at him sideways.

Halfway back to Bali's makeup table the assistant stopped and said, "Oh, somebody must be pretending to be Marilyn Monroe. Is this for real?"

Bali turned toward the door and a lovely, shapely leg came into view at the doorway, and the owner of the limb stepped into the green room. She removed her scarf, and tossed her blond curls and she then removed her dark glasses. She was dressed in a white Ivy League blouse with the collar turned up with the top two buttons unfastened. Her tight skirt had a slit up the side revealing a lovely leg.

The assistant looked back at Bali when she slipped into the dressing room. "It *is* Marilyn!" Bali gasped. This was one celebrity who didn't have to be explained to him.

"Yes, Darling, that's what *everybody* calls me."

Bali said of the experience, "We were completely frozen. Completely. I was absolutely numb." He didn't know whether to get up and shake her hand, so he just rose and stood in front of the beautiful lady.

After the initial shock, she asked Bali, "Will you come with me to have tea? Do you have time?"

"Of course I have time."

His helper asked, "May I join you?"

Bali said, "No"

Across the street from the theater was a ritzy hotel and they entered the restaurant off of the lobby. All of a sudden about 20 photographers and reporters materialized and were gathered around the entrance to the restaurant. Cameras clicked and lights flashed. She kicked Bali gently under the table and said, "When the waitress comes over, please don't say anything. Don't even talk."

"Okay."

"You know," Marilyn said sweetly with what Bali described as a twitter with hesitation between words, "my President called me. He said that I should come and see your performance wherever you were dancing." She seemed very shy.

"How did you like my performance?"

"Oh, it was just gorgeous. You looked magnificent. I have never seen Indian dance before and I am very grateful."

She asked him about his background. "Where were you born?"

"I was born in Nepal, in a village near Kathmandu."

"I've heard of Nepal and the Himalayas. Is it freezing there all the time?"

Bali let out a little laugh. "Not where I live. It is moderate in climate there. In fact, I performed for a king and a prince of Sikkim, and when the king asked me what I wanted, like an ass I told him to see the snow. My friend and sponsor, Desmond Doig, was furious at me because I didn't ask for jewels and land. I just wanted to see the snow."

Marilyn giggled and leaned across the table and touched his hand. "You are a sweet young man, Mr. Bali Ram. I am sure you will have a good life. I am sorry, but these reporters are hounding me. I am going to have to leave and I know I can trust you not to say a word to them. Just let them keep guessing." She wrapped up their tea time with, "I will tell my President that I met you and that we had a nice afternoon."

He turned around to see all the reporters giving fifty and one hundred dollar bills to the waiter to find out who the hell this guy was that Marilyn seemed enamored with, and where the hell did he come from. Each time the waiter came to the table, she nudged Bali again and he stopped talking. The paparazzi couldn't find out who this gorgeous, mysterious man was, but they took a lot of pictures. After they had tea and talked a while, Marilyn and Bali rose and walked out as she whispered, "Now don't utter a word to the reporters."

She left with a barrage of reporters snapping photos and asking questions as she slipped into the car waiting for her.

It was like a dream. He could not relax his energy was so high. Who could he talk to? What could he say? His manager had already left for the night. He was alone in the hotel room with no one to share a monumental moment with Marilyn Monroe.

After that amazing encounter, Bali began performing in all the states in the union, even Maui, Hawaii. He had already toured the world three times.

Bali no longer travelled with his troupe. Since they did not have work visas he had been paying all of their expenses: hotels, three meals a day, and medical expenses if they became sick. Instead, he recorded the music for his dance.

November 22, 1963, the news was broadcast around the world. President Kennedy had been shot and did not survive. Bali said he could not sleep for ten days. He was glued to the television day and night. He didn't even go the Martha Graham Dance School even though they kept calling him. He said he was very sick and that he was very sorry but he could not dance. He remembered Kennedy as one of the most important people he had met in his travels. Kennedy and Mother Teresa. Bali could not get over the tragic and senseless death of Kennedy. The nation and his family mourned along with Bali.

Marilyn died in August of 1962, 15 months before Kennedy.

John D. Rockefeller III

Bali told me, "Yes, I was world famous and I was involved in my thing and I never read newspaper too well. To be very honest with you, for 24 hours a day I was dancing." While touring he met many world leaders. In New York he met and was friends with John D. Rockefeller III, who had given Bali a grant to train with Martha Graham. He visited Bali at his Manhattan apartment, usually dressed in casual attire. It worried Bali for his security, and he told him, "John, I heard you are a very famous person but I cannot protect you. I am living in an apartment."

"Bali, look out the window."

Bali went to his window, and looked down at the street below. There were two men on the sidewalk at the corner, dressed in black suites and scanning the foot and vehicular traffic. Bodyguards! Rockefeller said, "You don't have to worry about that," meaning that Bali did not have to protect him. He was well taken care of.

John D. was the eldest son of John D. Rockefeller, Jr., who had five other children including Nelson. Bali's friend was involved with a bitter struggle with his brother Nelson over the control of Rockefeller Center and with his father over politics, particularly the anti-Semitic and racist policies. In addition to his interest in philanthropy, Rockefeller III made major commitments to supporting organizations related to East

Asian affairs, including the Asia Society, where Bali performed for him.

In 1956 John D. Rockefeller III established The Asia Society, initially to promote greater knowledge of Asia in the U.S.   Currently the Society is a global institution - with offices throughout the U.S. and Asia - that fulfills its educational mandate through a wide range of cross-disciplinary programming. As economies and cultures have become more interconnected, the Society's programs have expanded to address Asian American issues, the effects of globalization, and pressing concerns in Asia including human rights, the status of women, and environmental and global health issues such as HIV/AIDS.

According to their website, "The Asia Society defines the region of Asia as the area from Japan to Iran, from central Asia to Australia, New Zealand and the Pacific Islands. The Asia Society is a non-profit, non-partisan organization whose aim is to build awareness about Asian politics, business, education, arts, and culture through education. The organization sponsors the exhibitions of art, performance, film, lectures, and programs for students and teachers. The programs are aimed at increasing knowledge of society with a focus on human rights, environment, global health and the position of women."

Bali played a DVD for us at my son's house, made from a poor video recording at the Asia Society in New York City.   There was an introduction by two people who were being interviewed explaining the Society prior to introducing Bali Ram. At the time they said, "There were more people in India than the whole of

Africa and Latin America combined. Asia is the home of all great religions of the world and the great frameworks of our century including our own Christian religion.… Here we have the Hindu tradition, the Buddhist tradition, the Islamic tradition, and the tradition of Confucius in China, which is the framework within which people view themselves and each other and this is what they are blind about. The purpose of the Society is to make people aware of the other societies."

The narrator of the video at the Asia Society said that the building was located at 112 E 54th Street. Bali began his artistic dance while Rockefeller was sitting in the audience enjoying the performance.

The black and white recording couldn't show the splendor of his fuchsia and gold costume. He began by exaggerated eye movements, his eyes appearing enlarged by his black eye liner. His head moved back and forth and then he began tapping each foot to the rhythm of the exotic music so that the ankle bells constantly rang. His arms extended for the *mudras* to be expressed by his arms, his hands. and his fingers. He ended his performance by kneeling on his left knee, extending his right leg to the side with his toes pointed upward and his arms mimicking the legs. His grace and youthfully perfect body were a wonder to behold.

After the video, Bali reflected, "It's a funny thing. I didn't know how much power, how much money these people had. Have you read about him? He was blown up with a bomb, John D. the third?"

In researching his death I found no report of a bomb, only that he died in an automobile accident in Mount Pleasant, New York, near the Rockefeller family estate in1978, but Bali insisted that the accident that killed his friend included foul play.

Martin Luther King, Jr.

Bali was on a bus in New York City coming from the Martha Graham Dance Academy. Some men were standing by the bus stop near the back of Yankee Stadium near 8th Avenue, and Bali got off one block from the stadium. One of the men was wearing a white Gandhi hat, so Bali said to himself, "Wow! I'd like to have that hat. What store in New York did he buy this hat?" It was only a block from his bus stop so he walked back and approached the group of distinguished looking black men.

"Excuse me, Sir. Which store you get that hat?" he asked the well dressed man. "I would like to have one like it."

"I am sorry, but I didn't buy it from a store. I am a disciple of Gandhi so I got it from his ashram."

Bali was surprised that he was a disciple of Mahatma Gandhi, "Oh, I am sorry. I thought you got the hat from Macy's or Bloomingdale's."

"No," King said laughing. "I am not able to help you get one like this in New York."

"Sir, you look familiar to me. May I ask your name?"

"Martin Luther King."

"I've heard your name, but I don't believe I've met you."

King said, "Yes, I know we haven't met. I would have remembered you." And then he said, "I am giving a speech tonight at the Apollo Theater. I'd like you to come. What is your name?"

"My name is Bali Ram," and King wrote it down. As they talked briefly, King introduced Bali to his companions. "I'd like you to meet Reverend Abernathy and Mr. Whitney Young." After the introductions, King continued, "I will give your name to the people at the door and there will be chairs reserved for you and a guest in the front."

Bali sat in the front row and listened to King's speech announcing that he was organizing a march in Alabama, and he was asking people to join him. On April 13, 1963, the Birmingham campaign was launched. This would prove to be the turning point in the war to end segregation in the South. Bali went back stage after the speech and King was with a small black woman. "Bali, I would like to introduce you to Rosa Parks."

"Oh, how nice to meet you. My name is Bali Ram." Bali didn't know who she was at the time.

King was a Baptist minister who was drawn to Mahatma Gandhi for his philosophy of nonviolence. "As I read, I became deeply fascinated by his campaigns of nonviolent resistance. As I delved deeper into the philosophy of Gandhi, my skepticism concerning the power of love gradually diminished, and I came to see for the first time its potency in the area of social reform."

King had believed that "turn-the-other-cheek" philosophy and the "love-your-enemies" philosophy were only valid when individuals were in conflict with other individuals. When racial groups and nations were in conflict, a more realistic approach seemed necessary. "But after reading Gandhi, I saw how utterly mistaken I was."

In 1959 King made a pilgrimage to India. There he met with members of Gandhi's family, and with

Prime Minister Jawaharlal Nehru, who for decades had been a key ally of Gandhi in the struggle for Indian independence.

The intent of King's marches and rallies was to provoke mass arrests at such a level that it would "create a situation so crisis-packed that it will inevitably open the door to negotiation," in regards to equal rights and bring about anti-discrimination legislation.

Whitney Young Jr. at that time was the Executive Director of the National Urban League and he was President of the National Urban League from 1961 until his death in 1971. Young described his proposals for integration, social programs, and affirmative action in his two books, *To Be Equal* (1964) and *Beyond Racism*.

Ralph David Abernathy, Sr. was a leader of the American Civil Rights Movement, a minister, and a close associate of King. He earned a Masters' of Science degree at Alabama State University after serving in the United States Army during World War II. As an officer of the Montgomery, Alabama NAACP, he organized the first mass meeting for the Montgomery bus boycott to protest Rosa Parks' arrest on December 1, 1955. Abernathy and King went to school together in Atlanta, a partnership that ended with his lifelong friend's death on April 4, 1968. King said at the beginning of his last speech, "I've been to the mountain top," and that "Ralph David Abernathy is the best friend that I have in the world."

Rosa Parks with King, 1955

One day in 1943, at age 30, Rosa Parks boarded a bus in Montgomery, Alabama, and paid the fare. She then moved to her seat in the back rows that were considered the "colored" section. The driver, James Blake, told her to follow city rules and that she must get off the bus and re-enter from the back door. Rosa exited the bus, but before she could re-board at the rear door, Blake drove off, leaving her to walk home in the pouring rain.

Twelve years later in 1955, at age 42, Rosa had again boarded a bus, paid her fare and seated herself in the designated section. As all the white-only seats filled and two or three people were standing, the driver, who coincidentally happened to be James Blake again, demanded that four black people give up their seats to the white passengers. Years later, in recalling the events of the day, Parks said, "When that white driver stepped back toward us, when he waved his hand and ordered us up and out of our seats, I felt a determination cover my body like a quilt on a winter night."

Blake demanded, "Y'all better make it light on yourselves and let me have those seats." Three of them complied.

Parks said, "The driver wanted us to stand up, the four of us. We didn't move at the beginning, but he says, 'Let me have these seats.' And the other three people moved, but I didn't." The black man sitting next to her gave up his seat.

Parks moved, but toward the window seat; she did not get up to move to the re-designated colored section.

Blake asked Rosa, "Why don't you stand up?"

"I don't think I should have to stand up."

Blake called the police to arrest Parks. When recalling the incident for *Eyes on the Prize,* a 1987 public television series on the Civil Rights Movement, Parks said, "When he saw me still sitting, he asked if I was going to stand up, and I said, 'No, I'm not.' And he said, 'Well, if you don't stand up, I'm going to have to call the police and have you arrested.' I said, "You may do that."

Several months after her arrest, during a 1956 radio interview with Sydney Rogers in West Oakland, Rosa said she had decided, "I would have to know for once and for all what rights I had as a human being and a citizen."

Around the World Three Times

Desmond Doig acted as Bali's agent for some events around the world. As a famous, well respected, and very influential reporter, he was invited to embassies of many countries, making contact with ambassadors, consulates, and world dignitaries. This provided the platform to book Bali or hook him up with performances all over the globe.

Bali told me, "I was in Paris, London, Moscow, Yugoslavia, Mexico, and Maui, returning to an apartment in New York, or returning to India.

"I was in Africa, in Sudan, and in Tokyo, but I did not perform there. I was in New Zealand. I was in Germany. I was in New York.

"I used to do fifty-two performances in New York in one month, and get ten grand for each one at that time." He began his world tours solo with his magnificent costumes and his recorded music.

"I've been to all the states of the union in America. All of the states. I went to Cuba."

I asked him if Castro attended.

"I just perform right away, because I been booked. I had no contact with Castro or his brother or his soldiers, or anybody. It was a school, like a teaching school in Havana. One show in Cuba. I usually do one show each country. Many times I do two or three shows in same university in USA. Mostly I performed at colleges, universities and elementary schools in America. I was in World's Fair in Canada. I think it was in '67 in

Montreal." It was referred to as The 1967 International and Universal Exposition or Expo 67. It is considered to be the most successful World's Fair of the 20th century, with the most attendees to that date with 62 nations participating. It also set the single-day attendance record for a world's fair, with 569,500 visitors on its third day.

According to Sukanya Rahman, Indrani Rahman's daughter, Bali toured with Indrani in her dance company. Sukanya said, "Her (mother's) first U. S. tour with Bali in her troupe was 1960. She took him with her troupe to tour Europe and the U.S. in 1961. The U.S. tour was arranged by the Asia Society in New York. They also performed in Cuba for Castro and Che Guevera and Alicia Alonso. Also in Trinidad and Surinaam and Jacob's Pillow. Nehru invited my mother and her company including Bali to perform at the Indian Embassy in Washington, D. C. for President Kennedy and his family in 1961.

"Bali was a beautiful, elegant dancer. He and my mother were stunning on stage together. I vividly remember them dancing the *Geetam* and a *Jatiswarm* together. He also performed in her *Kuchipudi* dance drama episodes."

Bali said that people thought Indrani and he were lovers because they were always together. She was always with Bali. She was married to an architect and had a son and a daughter. They got along very well. If anything happened, an ambassador called, or a benefit or somebody was performing she was always calling him to go together.

Bali was given a difficult time even walking along the street I New York City with Indrani because she was Miss India and people would approach him offering huge sums of money to introduce them to Indrani. "What do you think I am, a pimp?" he would respond back, indignantly, "She's my friend, my dance partner. Why are you approaching me like this? Go to hell. Take your money and shove it."

When she would visit Bali, there was such a crowd that she had difficulty in going out. She was very striking woman. "People would flock to her. She would cause (auto) accidents. They came to her in restaurants," Bali said. He was young and he was being offered a few thousand of dollars for an introduction. "She's not my girlfriend. She's just my partner and she has just come to visit." Bali said, "She was a witch, a white witch. She could chew you up in a second."

When he was in Bombay, the movie actors and actresses were friendly with him and they would tell him that if he brought Indrani they could give him a good part in the movie. He said, "I only came to Bombay to dance, not to be a movie actor. I don't like making movies. I don't want to be an actor." He said he could have been as rich as a maharaja by now taking money from people who wanted to meet her. "That's not what I am for. I am for my heart and I am for my friend."

In Europe women were wild over him and very often made indecent proposals, asking him to make love to them, and to sleep with them to sire a baby. He said some had told him they had left their husbands for him. It is possible that he has many unintended offspring in Europe. He was very embarrassed by the advances and, as a gentleman, has never discussed intimate details about any women.

Bali was visiting London and Jawaharlal Nehru's sister, Vijaya Lakshmi Pandit, invited him to have tea at the Indian Embassy.   She served as the Indian ambassador to Ireland from 1955 until 1961, and was the commissioner to United Kingdom.   Her brother was the first prime minister of India.

"Bali, the Queen of England was in India.   Were you able to see her or meet her while she was there?" Ambassador Pandit asked him.

He said it was so out of the blue and that he really wasn't thinking right, when he responded, "Oh no. I am so busy preparing to come here and get things together on my own.   I didn't have time to see the Queen."

All the public had lined up on the street when the queen was in India, and it was a very important event. This was the time that she visited as mentioned in the Yeti scalp incident.

"Oh, my goodness!" she scolded.   "One should not be so very busy to not have time for Her Majesty, the Queen of England."

"And then," Bali told me, "it hit me finally when we were having tea, that I should never be so busy to ignore the Queen.   So that's what happened.   It was so funny."

Photos of Bali

Bali on a billboard ad in India for toothpaste
Photo by New Zealand Photographer, Brian Brake

Taken in India
Photo by New Zealand Photographer Brian Brake

Bali and Dancer
Photo by Desmond Doig

In India, Photo by George Blaker

Desmond Gave Bali a Birthday Party
at Hotel Janpath In New Delhi

Indrani Rahman & Bali Ram, Photo by © Habib Rahman

Bali at border between Nepal and India wearing
Tibetan Hat and Shirt, Photo by Desmond Doig

Bali Ram, age 77, Bend, Oregon, U.S.A
By Daniel Biggs, Jr.

Bali's Cooking Classes

L+ — food fashions family furnishings — THE NEW YORK TIMES, 1

DINING A L'INDIENNE: Bali Ram, a professional dancer who also enjoys preparing dishes indigenous to India such as dahl, rice garnished with green pepper and tomato, poppadums and lamb curry.

Nepalese's Favorite Restaurant Is His Own Home

By JEAN HEWITT

The New York Times, Thursday, March 11, 1965
By Jean Hewitt

"Why eat out when you can cook," was the answer Bali Ram, a dancer, gave to the question, "Which is your favorite restaurant?"

Mr. Ram, a native of Nepal, believes that the culture of a country is shown through its music, dancing, art, literature — and cooking. He demonstrated his belief last fall by giving a series of cooking classes at Asia House under the title "The Culture of India through Its Cookery."

After performing the classical dances of India for a young peoples' series at Lincoln Center, Mr. Ram found a release from tension by cooking at the classes held later on the same day, he said.

While recently preparing a typical Indian dinner for eight friends, Mr. Ram announced in his softly spoken, accented English, "I never get annoyed with cooking and I never say 'no' to preparing dinner for a group of fellow artists or friends."

Mr. Ram, a small, lithe, muscular young man with large sad eyes, dressed as carefully to prepare the dinner as he would to perform the ritualistic dances of his country. He was wearing a *dhotl* (sari-like loin cloth), *kurta* (long tunic-like coat) and *chappels* (embroidered sandals).

Precise Preparation

Preparation of the five main dishes was started in order of the length of time required to cook each, and with the precision and deftness that is an integral part of a dancer's training.

All ingredients for each dish were assembled in little piles around a chopping board as a small paring knife (Mr. Ram's favorite kitchen tool) reduced onion, buds of garlic, green beans, celery and other vegetables into neat, cross-cut pieces with a rhythm and accuracy made possible only by long practice. "From a child, always I liked neat slices, all the same size whether vegetables or other foods," he explained.

After two hours of kitchen preparation, Mr. Ram emerged calm, spotless, happy and proud to serve the dinner in the traditional Indian manner.

A large copper pot of rice was passed first (Indians are proud of their cooking utensils and serve many foods directly from the pan). The rice was plain boiled with no salt added.

Rice Covers Plate

Each guest was invited to cover his entire plate (in India a large leaf is used) with rice. Then four dishes — a vegetable curry, mince sag, lamb curry and dahl — were passed in succession and a portion of each placed atop the rice in a circle.

All these dishes were quite heavily salted and spiced, but this was counterbalanced by the bland rice. No salt is ever added at the table.

Poppadums (thin crisp wafers made from lentil flour), lightly browned and heated over a direct flame, were passed. Poppandums are available from Trinacria, 415 Third Avenue and the Kalustyan Trading Company, 397 Third Avenue. (Terrie's note: remember this was 1965).

Mr. Ram had taken care not to touch the dahl or the vegetable curries with the spoons used for the meat dishes in dererence to one of his country-women who is a strict vegetarian.

A curd drink based on yogurt accompanied the meal, and fresh fruit was the dessert.

Curry is cooling, according to Mr. Ram, much the same way as tea, and he enjoys repeating the belief held by many Indians that curry helps sinuses and colds. He uses imported, Madras-style curry powder (Sun Brand, also available from the Triancria and Kalustyan) supplemented by ginger root, cloves, turmeric and peppercorns.

Some of Mr. Ram's former cooking class pupils have persuaded him to plan and supervise the preparation of Indian dinners for them and to perform representative dances following the repast. Mr. Ram has completed three world tours, performed twice at the United Nations as well as before the late President John F. Kennedy on the occasion of the late Pandit Nehru's visit to Washington, under the State Department's American-Asia cultural exchange program.

Recipes follow for four of the Indian dishes Mr. Ram served at the dinner. (End of article).

Shala Mattingly knew first hand that Bali was a wonderful cook. She said that the cooking course at the Asia Society was in the old building on the east side. The new building is on Park Avenue. They all would dig in and help preparing and cleaning up afterwards in the kitchen. Bali went out front and did the teaching the demonstration to the people. He did all the cooking, but the others helped in the chopping and the preparation of the vegetables, and then afterwards, there was tons of washing up. She said, "It was most enjoyable and I wish that he could do more of that."

Recipes from the New York Times Article

Dahl

The recipes serve 8

(Described as the oldest of peasant foods is sometimes spelled dal)

¼ cup cooking oil

I onion, cut into quarters and sliced

4 gloves garlic, finely chopped

2 tablespoons finely chopped fresh ginger root (he never peels it)

2 bay leaves, chopped

8 whole cloves

8 whole black peppercorns

6 cherry tomatoes, halved or two tomatoes, quartered

4 tablespoons imported Madras-style curry powder

I teaspoon turmeric

6 ¼ cups water, approximately

I ½ pounds lentils (those with a reddish cast are preferred over the deep green-colored ones)

2 ½ teaspoons salt

     I.   Heat the oil in a deep, heavy 3 to 4 quart pan until hot. Add onion and fry until lightly browned. Add garlic, ginger, bay leaves, cloves and peppercorns and cook I minute. Add the tomatoes and continue cooking.

     2.   Mix the curry powder and turmeric with one-quarter cup of the water.

3.   Add curry powder mixture to the pan and cook, while stirring, 3 minutes, adding a tablespoon of water if necessary to prevent sticking.

4.   Add the cleaned, drained lentils and the salt and cook 2 minutes. Add remaining water. Bring to a boil, cover and simmer about I hour, or until the lentils are tender and the liquid is absorbed. More water may be added during cooking if necessary.

Meat Marinade
(not in article)

Note from Bali Ram for Curries: if possible marinate lamb, pork or chicken as follows:

I tablespoon arrowroot

I tablespoon soya sauce

I tablespoon oil

Mix together and rub on the meat.

For pork or lamb add a little water and rub on meat. Prick the meat with a fork. Marinate overnight when possible.

Brown the meat before adding to the recipes

Lamb Curry

½ cup cooking oil
1 onion, quartered and sliced
3 large cloves garlic, finely chopped
1 tablespoon finely chopped fresh ginger root
2 bay leaves, chopped
6 whole cloves
12 whole black peppercorns
1 ½ inch pieces of whole cinnamon stick
6 cherry tomatoes, halved, or two tomatoes, quartered
4 ½ tablespoons imported Madras-style curry powder
1½ teaspoons turmeric
1 tablespoon paprika
¼ cup water
3 pounds boneless lamb cubes, cut from the leg or shoulder
  1½ to 2 tablespoons salt

1.   Heat the oil in a heavy skillet or pan. Fry the onion in it until lightly brown; add garlic, ginger, bay leaves, cloves, peppercorns, cinnamon and tomatoes and cook 2 minutes.

2.   Mix the curry powder with the turmeric, paprika and water and add to the pan.

3.   Cook, stirring about 3 minutes over high heat, adding a tablespoon or two of water to prevent sticking if necessary.

4.   Add the meat and the salt and cook, stirring 1 minute. Cover and cook over medium heat about 30 minutes, or until the meat is tender. No liquid is added, the liquid comes out of the meat to make the sauce as it cooks.

Vegetable Curry

1/3 cup oil
1 onion, quartered and sliced
2 cloves garlic, finely chopped
1 tablespoon fresh ginger root, finely chopped
1 bay leaf, chopped
6 whole peppercorns
3 whole cloves
2 cups small cauliflower flowerets
2 cups small broccoli flowers
1 ½ cups sliced Chinese cabbage
1 sweet red pepper, diced (hot red pepper may be used if desired)
1 green pepper, diced
1 ½ cups roughly diced celery
1 cup green beans, sliced crosswise
1 tablespoon salt
3 tablespoons imported Madras-style curry powder
1 tablespoon turmeric
¼ cup water

1.   Heat oil in a large heavy pan. Add the onion and fry until lightly browned. Add garlic, ginger, bay leaf, peppercorns, cloves and vegetables.
2.   Cook over high heat, stirring for 10 minutes. Add the salt.
3.   Mix the curry powder, turmeric and water together and add. Cook over high heat, stirring constantly, until oil starts to separate, about 5 minutes. Cover and cook until vegetables are crisp-tender. A small amount of water may be needed to prevent sticking.

Mince Sag

1/3 cup cooking oil
1 onion, quartered and sliced
3 cloves garlic, finely chopped
1 tablespoon finely chopped fresh ginger root
6 whole cloves
6 whole black peppercorns
6 cherry tomatoes, halved, or two tomatoes, quartered
2 tablespoons turmeric
¼ cup water
1 pound ground lamb or ground round of beef
1 tablespoon salt
20 ounces of spinach, washed and chopped (Terrie's note: I used apx. 12 ounces).

1.   Heat the oil in a large heavy skillet or pan. Fry the onion in it until lightly browned. Add garlic, ginger, cloves, peppercorns, and tomatoes and cook 2 minutes.
2.   Mix the turmeric with the water and add to the pan. Cook, stirring, 3 minutes. Add the meat and salt; cook 5 minutes.
3.   Add the spinach, cover and cook rapidly until the spinach is cooked. No extra water is needed. Stir occasionally to prevent sticking.

Bali's Manager

At the side of the Carnegie Hall building was a newspaper stand. The advertisement was in the newspaper that Bali Ram and Company was going to perform at one of the stages at Carnegie Hall. After he ate lunch, Bali left his hotel to get a newspaper at the stand. A Latino man had come from his acting class as Bali picked up the newspaper.

The man said, "You must be Bali Ram."

"Yes, I am. How do you know?"

"Well, I saw your picture in the newspaper. My name is Gregory Sierra."

"How do you do? It is very nice to meet you, Gregory."

They chatted for a few minutes and Sierra said, "Bali, I would like you to meet my acting teacher, Bill Haines."

"Oh, sure."

"His studio is only two blocks away from here. If you would walk down there, you will meet him."

"Okay. I can do that."

Sierra gave Bali the address. "I will be seeing you soon and I will come to your concert."

"Thank you."

Gregory Sierra played Sergeant Amenguale on *Barney Miller*, and Julio Fuentes as the Puerto Rican neighbor on *Sanford and Son*. He guest starred on *All in the Family*, he was also a cast member on *Miami Vice* and has had regular roles on TV shows including *Zorro and Son, Something is Out There* and *Common Law.*

Bali walked down the street slowly, and he was really not looking for the studio, but there it was. The door was open and people were going in and out and the address matched. He said to himself, "This must be it." The owner and acting coach, who went by the name of Bill Haines, was busy with about twenty people in the class. Bali went in quietly and sat down. He noticed that everyone was staring at him. He was wearing his traditional Indian clothing the *kurta and dhoti* (like pajamas) and slippers, all his rings and a vest. He had long hair to his shoulders.

Everyone left when the class was over and Bill wiped his sweaty face with a towel, turned around and said, "Oh! You're still here. Can I help you? My name is Bill Haines."

"Oh. Your student Gregory Sierra sent me to you. My name is Bali Ram."

"Gee. I have heard your name somewhere." Bali showed him the newspaper and he said, "Oh my God. It's very nice to meet you. You're a dancer, right?"

"Yes, I will be performing tonight at Carnegie Hall."

"I would like to come to your show, if it's alright."

Bali said, "Sure. I think I can reserve two seats in the front for you. Just tell them at the door that you are a guest of mine."

"Okay," Haines said. He and Sierra went to the performance enjoying front row seats. Afterwards Haines told Bali he could not believe that he could dance for two and a half hours. What endurance!

He was also dancing at Lincoln Center where all of the people in Haines's class came to see his performance. Bali said that Lincoln Center was full of students from local colleges and universities. It was packed. After the performance Bali told Haines, "I hope you don't mind, but I have to leave. I give cooking classes at the Asia House." *The New York Times* had promoted his cooking classes, so from the Lincoln Center performance, he had to go directly to the Asia House.

"Do you mind if we come along?"

"How many people are you bringing along?" Bali asked.

"Just me and Greg Sierra."

"Sure, you can come."

Haines and Sierra went to Bali's cooking class, and they waited around and tasted the aromatic and delicious food that Bali prepared. The attendees of the class, about 30 or 40, were lawyers, judges, accountants, and nurses. It was well received. He held classes weekly for about a year.

Haines' last name at birth was Prock. Haines was his theatrical name. He was interested in Bali and said, "If you don't mind, I'd like to organize your lighting and your props on the stage. I am an acting teacher, but I have a lot of experience with lighting." Haines was excited and happy and expressed to Bali that he had found a precious jewel. Thus began a 25-year association. Haines gave up his studio to become Bali's full time manager and stage director.

Bill Haines at Agra, India
Photo by Shala Mattingly

To Bali he looked Italian. Haines was heavy set, and very intelligent. He just loved the theater life. Bali thought that Haines was a good manager. He knew how to fix the lighting. He knew which entrance Bali should come on the stage. He knew where Bali should stand. "If Bali Ram is moving, I want amber lights on him," he would direct the stage crew. Haines was a gifted stage manager and also organized his U.S. tours.

Haines never married. His mom and dad were divorced and his mom lived in New York at that time. Bali and Haines lived in Manhattan at the unbelievable monthly rate of $65 for this apartment.

Handsome and sexually active, according to Bali, Haines "picked up girls like flies," Bali said and brought them home to his mother's house. Bali didn't want his overnight ladies at his place.

Haines was an ex-soldier having served in the Army during Vietnam. He was abrupt, loud, and often obnoxious. Bali at times was afraid of his temper and that he would go after Bali.

Haines became overweight and it worried Bali for his health. Haines would say, "Don't talk to me today, Bali. I have a problem," meaning with his health.

He took a pill for diabetes and they tested his blood sugar every day. He was good to Bali in so many ways, "father, mother, watch dog." But Bali was just afraid that he would tear somebody apart. He was sometimes afraid to walk with him on the street and he told him many times, "Bill, please control your temper. I don't like it. If you're going to do that, I am not going to go with you." Sometimes Haines was not able to control his temper. Bali thought it might have had something to do with serving in Vietnam. It was likely that his blood sugar level and poor diet contributed to his tirades.

Bali wondered why Haines would want to stay with him because they argued so often. Haines realized that Bali had no one to do the stage production and lighting, so he took on the responsibility. After the shows, he wouldn't let anyone into the dressing room until Bali removed his makeup and changed his clothes.

Bali would get upset about Haines's eating habits and Haines would pound his fist on the table so hard that the flower vase would fall on the floor. "Don't tell me what to do," he would holler. Two or three times he grabbed Bali by the neck and threw him into the wall.

"Please leave. You don't have to do this," Bali pleaded. "I really don't need a manager and we can still be friends. We can visit each other but you are free to go."

In New York Bali had come back from Martha Graham's class. Bali's friend, Shala Mattingly, who met Bali in Delhi while a student of North Indian dance, had moved to New York and lived in an apartment on the same floor as Bali and Bill on 52nd Street. Mattingly was sitting in the living room. Bali opened the rice that Haines was cooking and put his finger in the pot to check the doneness, and he said, "Haines, the rice is not done yet."

Haines was obviously in a foul mood, and he picked up a cleaver. Bali saw Haines coming towards him wielding the cleaver and he ran out the door and down the stairs and onto the sidewalk with Haines running after him, knife in hand. Mattingly was looking out the window, terrified, to view the scene below. Haines couldn't catch Bali because Bali was young and fast, as people on the street watched this mad man chasing Bali. Haines went back to the apartment, muttering to himself, "Who the hell does he think he is? He can cook his own food," as he began a new batch of rice.

Mattingly recalled Haines' rages. She had met him while Bali was still at his academy and they had a lot of good times together in India.

Haines took care of Bali in all ways. Bali said Haines was somewhere between a mother and a security guard. He was very protective of Bali. If a caller came, he wanted to know who they were, why they were they coming to visit, what they did for work, what was their living situation, and he asked for their phone number. He monitored everything in Bali's life.

Haines wore Indian clothes when he stayed with Bali at his house in New Delhi, India.

While attending the academy, Bali rented an apartment in Nizamuddin in Delhi. Mattingly visited many times and does not recall Bali's house in New Delhi.

At his house, Bali had Indian servants and thought at times they loved Haines more than him. But Haines was afraid he would catch a disease and didn't mingle or make friends there. However, they did go ballroom dancing on occasion and Haines would dance with ladies. He also rode the trains with Bali in third class and seemed to relish observing the people and the flavor of India.

Bill Haines at Bali's House
New Delhi, India

Haines didn't go to Paris when Bali performed but he stayed in India. Bali said it was probably a money shortage and he was only going for one week.

Haines' foul mouth, and his blunt, honest opinions, seemed a direct contrast to Doig's British mannerisms. Opposites attract. Doig and Haines got along well, and they laughed all the time. "Will you two please stop. You are laughing so hard I am afraid something will happen to you," Bali pleaded, while being very content that the two enjoyed each other so much. Doig invited Bali and Haines from Delhi to Calcutta to stay at his house. Both of them liked performances, opera, and to be entertained. Doig was a dance critic, according to Bali.

Haines and Bali were at Doig's house very often. That's why Doig felt comfortable turning the care of Bali over to Haines. Years later, when Bali was in Arizona, Bali went to Calcutta and Bill gave him a very thick letter for Doig asking Doig to take care of Bali and to have Bali learn new dances while he was there.

Author and fellow guest at Millbrook, Ted Druch, thought that "Haines snaked Bali (from Doig) and brought him back to the states." Bali declares it was a mutual decision and that the two men got along great.

At times Haines could be a bastard and butcher people with a few words and not even feel it. In India when people were talking next door, Haines would vault over the wall between houses and look at them and say gruffly, "What's happening?" scaring the neighbors while they apologized for disturbing him. In spite of his over-protectiveness and explosive temper, he could be very kind and he was very funny and made Bali laugh very often.

They lived in India for a few years. After returning to New York, Haines and Bali became involved in an ashram in Monroe. Haines dressed in Indian clothing and had collected Indian artifacts that he moved with him. He was considered one of the leaders of the ashram.

Jackie "O"

Jacqueline "Jackie" Lee Bouvier Kennedy, before she added "Onassis" to her name, sat with Adlai Stevenson II at the United Nations for Bali's second performance in 1965. Stevenson had been appointed by President Kennedy as the Ambassador to the United Nations from 1961 to 1965.

Bali danced as Haines explained the meaning of the *mudras* or hand gestures to the audience as he glided across the stage with bells ringing and exotic Indian music accompanying them in their colorful costumes. Jackie wrote Bali a lovely note, which was also signed by Stevenson. Bali said he framed it and left with a close friend in India, but his friend doesn't know where it is. He said it read something like:

It was very nice entertainment. You are a beautiful and handsome man as always, Bali Ram. I enjoyed your performance tremendously.

Sincerely,
Jacqueline Kennedy
Adlai Stevenson

It is a treasure that he lost, but the kind words still live in his heart.

Life with Leary

LSD. The drug of the 60's. The drug choice at Woodstock letting you "turn on, tune in, drop out," or as coined in the lyrics of a Jim Stafford song, "take a trip and never leave the farm," although I believe he was referring to marijuana. Timothy Leary, a well educated man, lecturing at Harvard, was the world's most prominent advocate of LSD, and also experimented with other psychedelic drugs. Bali was totally unaware of Leary's reputation when Leary approached Bali at the end of his performance in New York City, saying, "My name is Timothy Leary."

"How nice," was Bali's standard answer, "How are you?"

"I'm right on. Bali, your dance is magnificent."

"Thank you very much." Bali, Haines, and Leary became acquainted. Upon meeting Haines for the first time, Leary realized, according to Ted Druch's novel, *Madmen of Millbrook*, "This was just the guy to straighten out the mess that Leary made of his League for Spiritual Discovery. He arranged a meeting and Leary invited the ashram in Monroe (New York) to join him in Millbrook." The League of Spiritual Discovery was the name of the religion that Leary founded in order to have the right to use LSD that was given for the use of Peyote to Native Americans.

In Bali's account of the invitation, Leary said to him, "Come with me where I am living in Millbrook."

"Why you want me to go to Millbrook?"

"Oh, it is a beautiful place full of peaceful people. My family is staying there and I think you would love it." Leary introduced Bali to the Hitchcock fraternal twins, who owned the estate and Bali liked Billy and Tommy very much. Druch said **Tommy** was dark and brooding, and Billy was blond and lively. They both married beautiful women. Billy married a dark-haired Venezuelan beauty, Aurora. Tommy married, Suzanne, a lovely blond. Both had two children, one blond and one dark-headed. Leary and his followers lived in the main house, while the twins occupied the "bungalow" which, including gardens, an Olympic-sized swimming pool, and two tennis courts, filled a half of an acre on the Millbrook estate.

Bali said, "It sounds good to me." Bali and Haines went to live and experience bizarre and incredible events over the next couple of years.

Leary was born in 1920 in Massachusetts. An only child, he disappointed his father and mother, devout Catholics, by dropping out of Holy Cross College after two years. His father was a dentist in the military, holding an officer's rank. It pleased his father immensely when Leary was eligible for West Point, but he dropped out of there also. Leary did serve in World War II as a psychologist in a Pennsylvania hospital. He moved to Oakland, California, after he was discharged and went to the University of California at Berkeley and ultimately received a PhD in psychology. He was a professor at the University of California at San Francisco until a tragic event. On Leary's 30th birthday his wife was found in their garage, having committed suicide and leaving Leary with two grief-stricken children. He moved to

Europe for a time. When he returned to America, he began lecturing at Harvard University in New York.

In the summer, he rented a home in Mexico, and at 39 years old in 1960 another event occurred which changed his life and altered the culture of America forever as described at the time of his death in 1996 by an article published in the British newspaper *The Independent:*

In 1960, then aged 39, beside the swimming pool of his rented summer villa in Cuernavaca, Mexico, he ate a handful of odd-looking mushrooms which he had bought from the witch doctor of a nearby village. Within minutes, he was later to recall, he felt himself "being swept over the edge of a sensory niagara into a maelstrom of transcendental visions and hallucinations. The next five hours could be described in many extravagant metaphors, but it was above all and without question the deepest religious experience of my life."

On returning to Harvard he began experimenting on himself, his colleagues, and students with psilocybin, a chemical derivative of mushrooms with powerful mind-altering effects. He said he decided to "dedicate the rest of my life to the systematic exploration of this new instrument."

Leary was captivated by mind-altering substances. In spite of the fact that they were legal at that time, Harvard University asked him to resign. He made the acquaintance of the Hitchcock twins while at college, and they invited Leary to stay at the main house on their property in 1963 while he was experimenting, partying, and writing books. The house, known as the Millbrook Estate or Denheim Castle, was purchased by the boys' mother Margaret Mellon Hitchcock. Her father was William Larimer Mellon, who came from wealth and his family was mostly known for their Gulf Oil holdings. Other family interests included Alcoa, Westinghouse, H. J. Heinz, *Newsweek*, and U.S. Steel. Margaret married Thomas Hitchcock, Jr. They had four children, two of which were twins Billy (William) and Tommy (Thomas III).

Margaret's husband, usually called Tommy, had a very colorful career. He joined the Lafayette Flying Corps in France during World War I. He was shot down and captured by the Germans but escaped his captors by jumping out of a train. He hid in the woods during the daytime then walked more than one hundred miles for eight nights to the safety of Switzerland.

After the war, Tommy studied at Harvard University. Playing polo, he led the U.S. team to victory in the 1921 International Polo Cup. From 1922 to 1940, Hitchcock carried a 10-goal handicap, which is the highest ranking in polo, from the United States of America Polo Association. He led four teams to U.S. National Open Championships in 1923, 1927, 1935 and 1936. F. Scott Fitzgerald was inspired by Tommy and loosely based two characters in *The Great Gatsby* and *Tender is the Night* on him.

He was killed and buried in 1944 in England while testing a military aircraft serving as a Lieutenant Colonel in the U. S. Air Force in the Second World War.

The Gate House at Millbrook Estate

When Bali arrived at Millbrook, he was amazed as they drove up to the stone gatehouse which had a residence over it for the guards with a huge iron gate. It was a piece of art in itself. Maple trees lined the driveway to the house towering like a tunnel. The 2500-acre property was surrounded by nine miles of fencing. The main house was in the Victorian style with an enormous barn and stable complex. There were stone bridges and beautiful gardens, a bowling alley built like a chalet with an upstairs that housed guests, an underground swimming pool, and underground garden. The lawns were elegant. It was as grand as any European castle. There was also a place of worship called Grace Chapel. Bali said that while Leary was there, a psychedelic face was painted across the whole front of the house. He said it looked to him like a demon's face. Robert Greenfield, author of *Timothy Leary: A Biography*, said that Buddha's face was painted on the four story, sixty-four room mansion. It had two round towers, a redbrick chimney, against the white house, and a wide veranda. Greenfield said of the interior, "The woodwork was hand carved. The tapestries on the dining room walls were elegant but fading. The ceilings were inlaid with wooden panels. There was a music room, an aquarium room, ten bathrooms, and a hotel-size kitchen with a walk-in refrigerator..." The style of decoration was described as "Bavarian baroque."

Bali was a guest in the wing to the left of the house which was a huge, round turret. The bathrooms were luxurious. The living room had a grand fireplace of the finest marble. It was a place where the guests of that wing gathered.

Also living in the guest wing were Leary's son, who went by Jack or Jackie and Richard Alpert who was later given the spiritual name of Baba Ram Das while in India. Alpert cared for the two neglected children of Leary, even paying for dental work. Jack had been quoted as saying about his father, "He was pretty much always totally inept at being a father to me and Susan. Actually, he would sometimes moan about us as the millstones around his neck."

There were many marriages and many parties. Bali told me that he never saw Leary take LSD or drugs, but that he was a raving alcoholic, which might account for the fact that Leary never seemed to care where his teenage children were or what they were doing.

Susan lived in the main house with Leary, who was involved with different women while living there, including the Hitchcocks' sister, Peggy, who was fourteen years younger than Leary. Peggy was described as "a real Bohemian, but also the sweetest and nicest person in the family." At that time, Peggy's mother, whom her children called "Mumma," was thrilled that she was seeing a Harvard professor, as her mother didn't approve of her previous boyfriend. Mumma would later realize that, in spite of Leary's pedigree, he would not have been a fit for Peggy, whose heart was broken when she was thrown aside for Nena van Schlebrugge, a beautiful high fashion model, whose mother was a Swedish baroness. (A side note: their marriage did not last much beyond their honeymoon and she ultimately married Robert Thurman and is the mother of actress Uma Thurman. In October of 2012, Uma gave her parents a granddaughter, who might just have one of longest American names I've heard: Rosalind Arusha Arkadina Altalune Florence Thurman-Busson, or "Luna" for short.)

Part of Leary's honeymoon was spent in India. He usually dressed in a long white tunic over white pants, wearing sandals and sat in the Lotus position. Leary was influenced by Indian garbs, Lamas, Indian texts, quest for enlightenment, and hashish.

Bali described the Hitchcocks' mother, Margaret, as wearing rags. He said it was hard to tell she was a billionaire. She used a walking stick. Her tennis shoes and dresses were torn and she didn't drive a luxury car.

Bali said, "She had so much money, she didn't care. She could buy anything or anybody if she wanted to."

She told him, "To hell with it all. I want to be me." Bali said she used to come up to him and kiss him on each cheek and she told him, "I'm so happy. My kids are so happy with you."

Margaret Hitchcock

Margaret did not live on her estate. Leary was the principle tenant at that time. Bali said there must have been about 50 of Leary's followers living there, also. Druch, in *Madmen of Millbrook* said, "Fifty people living there, more or less, sitting around on their keisters all day, stoned or not, was a recipe for boredom, and any feud, that might normally have nothing to do with more than a few people at most, could get blown into a major issue facing the community."

Leary received donations for his foundation to pay for living expenses while he enjoyed the rent-free estate, thanks to the Hitchcocks. Reporters were hovering constantly. Bali would watch the antics from his third floor porch shivering in his jacket while sunlight came into the porch as Leary and his guests were playing volleyball or basketball below, screaming, shouting, saying provocative things to each other which Bali described as "nasty things" while most of them were high and completely nude. Bali would never join in as he was shy and afraid of the scene below which he felt was mad with drugs. Many women just wanted Bali to get with them and he just couldn't live that lifestyle but was, at the same time, fascinated to observe it.

There were horse stables and one report said that the barn had large walls made of Italian marble. There was also a small waterfall on the property. The bowling alley had two regulation sized lanes with automatic pin changers.

The twins could access the swimming pool from their four bedroom bungalow that had a Japanese bath in the basement. The bungalow where Billy and Tommy both stayed was a 15 minute walk from the main house. Once in a while during their weekend getaway to Millbrook, the brothers invited Bali to dine with them - otherwise he ate in the main house. At the bungalow, Scottish cooks, servants and waiters dressed in suits, gloves and tuxedos. The cooks were crazy about this shy Nepalese, and brought him treats and special food – always fussing over him. According to Druch, Bali prepared many delicious Indian dishes for the residents.

The grounds were immaculately trimmed and kept clean. The Hitchcock family must have paid for the maintenance of the grounds. Leary used the estate to experiment on drugs. Behind the main house was a shed or small house that had been converted into a sort of temple for meditation. Behind that temple on the grounds was Lunacy Hill, where people went also to meditate.

One day Leary asked Bali, "I am putting on a show in Greenwich Village. It's called *The Birth of Buddha*. Would you like to dance in my show?"

"Sure. Why not."

There was a variety of performers in the show, and he wanted Bali to entertain. Leary had transformed the bowling alley at Millbrook into a "theater of light" using slide projectors modified to hold 1,000 watt light bulbs. This became so popular they moved the performances to Greenwich Village, and the Village Theater seated 2,000. These were attended by wealthy friends and associates of the Hitchcock twins "with chauffeurs waiting" to see the light show. Author Robert Greenfield said, "His (Leary's) psychedelic celebrations of the Lower East Side of New York served as a coming-out party for all the young and beautiful people in the city who had just begun getting high on LSD."

Bali went on stage in The Village to perform. It had a huge screen and Bali was behind the screen with a bright light shining on him towards the screen which illuminated his body and enlarged his image as a silhouette to the audience. He glided, lifting his legs and arms and hands into classic poses. The people loved it! They were screaming and applauding at the conclusion of his performance. How Bali wished he could have seen himself from the front of the stage while he listened to the cheers and bravos.

While living at Millbrook, Bali danced for Leary and his guests. He was mentioned in Greenfield's book as "dancing in full costume in the music room" on Thanksgiving Day in 1966. Ted Druch described Bali as, "His dancing was spectacular and so was his costume, a golden pleated skirt, over tight gold trousers. His bare, milk chocolate chest wore only a red string that crossed it from shoulder to waist. He had a magnificent physique."

There were no servants in the main house. Bali said that the followers helped to care for the house and grounds and that Leary received donations which funded his projects. One person described the kitchen as being filled with dirty dishes with cockroaches crawling all over the kitchen. Greenfield said, "For the month before Thanksgiving, the only reason people at Millbrook had been eating regularly was because beatnik poet and full-time resident, Diane DiPrima, had taken it upon herself to prepare three meals a day for as many as 50 people at a time." In fact she published a memoir entitled, "The Holidays at Millbrook – 1966." Tim could not even make it downstairs to eat dinner at his own table he was so lost in a high dose of acid.

After Bali's recital, Allen Ginsberg, who was an American poet and one of the leading figures of the Beat Generation in the 1950s, began chanting "Hare Krishna," while using his finger symbols. The Beat Generation included experimentation with drugs, alternative forms of sexuality, an interest in Eastern religion, a rejection of materialism, and uncensored expression in life and literature.

Bali recalled that once hordes of reporters from all over the world came to Millbrook to interview and report on Leary. He would not grant an interview that night and invited them to stay at Millbrook overnight. Leary said he would give them an interview in the morning at breakfast.

The reporters sat around the breakfast table, eating and drinking their morning coffee. Everybody was drinking coffee except Bali who knew what was about to happen, which he described in detail. "All the reporters, they started dancing and being funny. They go through emotions and make ass of themselves, and sometimes they play, sometimes they laugh, sometime they cry. There were women, too, almost 50 percent. But it was so funny. Women were taking their clothes off. It like a mad house! Timothy Leary bombed them all.

"All night long it went on like that. In the morning everybody came and sat at the table for breakfast. Everybody was laughing and they said, 'Timothy Leary! We're going to get you.' They ate with Timothy Leary and go back home. But then all wrote such beautiful articles about him." Is it any wonder all the reviews and articles were positive? They were all "bombed" by Leary.

Bali said he had tried LSD occasionally but emphatically said, "No! No, I would not take it that day. I knew what was going to happen. I used to see people freaking out on it so I don't want to make an ass of myself. I was scared." He was practicing his dancing all the time and he had to be clear and ready for a performance.

The Millbrook estate was described by Luc Sante of *The New York Times* as: "The headquarters of Leary and gang for the better part of five years, a period filled with endless parties, epiphanies and breakdowns, emotional dramas of all sizes, and numerous raids and arrests, many of them on flimsy charges concocted by the local assistant district attorney, G. Gordon Liddy."

In Robert Greenfield's *Timothy Leary: a Biography,* Jean McCready recalled, "When Tim was around, he and Bill Haines would take LSD and argue.

Raise their voices and yell at each other. Haines was not impressed or cowed by Tim. I couldn't believe how these men could take quantities of psychedelics and not blow their minds. Not get past their personality shit. But they didn't. They couldn't even agree to disagree."

Druch said that Leary was away from Millbrook for long periods of time and that Haines was in charge. Druch said, "Bill Haines was the son of a prominent Lutheran minister, and though he claimed to have become an atheist at ten, I didn't think he'd fully liberated himself from his, no doubt intense, early conditioning. His rebellion took the form of his own church, albeit a church that went out of its way to puncture religious superstitions and hypocrisy, using humor and satire as teaching tools.

"Haines had been with the forces that liberated the concentration camps. He served a year in the brig for assaulting an officer. He was a certified minister. He was a director in an off-Broadway playhouse. Possibly extorting money from his father, which he claimed was due him.

"Haines was the only one in the place who could keep his mind and sights on a goal, and work consistently towards it. He was a rock of consistency in a sea of changes, not that he couldn't be as maddening as the others at times, but he always exuded an air of plain good sense, something that was sorely missing among most of the members of the League."

On December 9, 1967, local cops arrested six Millbrook residents, Haines among them, and they spent the night in jail. While Haines was being loaded into the police van and handcuffed to one of the arrestees, Art Kleps blew his nose into a tissue and tossed it into the driveway. A deputy gathered the tissue for evidence and bagged it. The headline of Leary's account of the raid in *The East Village Other* read "The Great Millbrook Snot Bust." The arrest warrants charged Timothy Leary, Bill Haines, and Willam Hitchcock with conspiracy to create a public nuisance and criminal facilitation.

Bob Dylan and Woodstock

Having learned the art of pottery from Al Bonk, a resident of Millbrook and an accomplished potter, Bali and Bonk set up a kiln and potters' wheels at the Millbrook estate. Druch said, "Under Al's tutelage, Bali's artistic ability found a new expression in ceramics, and he did excellent work, even as a beginner." Tables were set up to decorate their stoneware. "Bali was more artistic, and some of the stuff he was producing was downright elegant, particularly after they'd mastered the art of porcelain." Other artwork included silk-screening, a sandal shop, and jewelry making.

On occasion Bali would get a ride to New York City with one of the visitors or groupies and take a box of his pottery into the city to sell. He had a grant from John D. Rockefeller III to study with Martha Graham and so he would go into the city to train.

He learned modern dance from Martha Graham, the greatest modern dancer in New York City, and he studied under her for two years in her 63rd Street studio. Originally he met her at 17 in Calcutta. Doig had thrown a party for Graham after she performed at the Lighthouse Theater in Calcutta, which is now a movie theater.

Martha Graham standing next to Bali
In New York City, New York, U.S.A.

Doig pitched to Graham, "We have a young male dancer, Bali Ram.   He is very shy, but is very accomplished."

Graham was very nice to Bali, and she responded directly to him, "Maybe someday you can come to my school"

Bali replied, "If God willing, it will happen." And there he was, one of her students. years later.

He also received dance lessons from Robert Joffrey at his school in New York. Joffrey was the founder and artistic director of the Joffrey Ballet, a company renowned for its wide-ranging repertory and exuberant young performers.

Every month or two Bali would go to the town of Woodstock to sell his unique artwork. At that time it was a very small village, with one narrow road running through it. Bali said that there wasn't room for the cars and someone to walk alongside the road at the same time. Shops were on one side and farms on the other. There was a hill across from the shops and over the hill was a river. There was one sheriff. It was while Bali was in the village of Woodstock that Bob Dylan, who lived there at the time, came to town. The two of them became friendly, and often had coffee together. When he came into the coffee shop, Dylan would have his guitar hanging by his fanny, and he wrote songs while Bali was visiting with him.

Bali said, "I thought he was just a kid, just like me. When he went home we used to throw rocks at each other. He lived up on the hill and I had a friend I used to visit there at the bottom of the hill. I would go to Woodstock and give my pottery to the shops for people to sell. On the weekends I would have a booth." His pottery would sell out quickly.

Bob Dylan's mentor was Joan Baez. At one time they were friends and lovers. She often invited him on stage during her concerts, getting him national and international prominence. In 1966, while living in Woodstock, Dylan crashed his motorcycle and didn't tour again for eight years, except a few select appearances. He then traveled to England for a rock festival on August 31, 1969, after rejecting offers to appear at the Woodstock Music & Art Fair in mid August. Dylan was one of the original inspirations for the festival, but he was unable to go because one of his children was in the hospital over that weekend.

The actual town for the event was Bethel, New York, on a 600-acre dairy farm, which lasted four days. Woodstock.com describes the festival as follows: "Woodstock is known as one of the greatest happenings of all time and — perhaps - the most pivotal moment in music history."

Joni Mitchell said, "Woodstock was a spark of beauty where half-a-million kids saw that they were part of a greater organism."

According to Michael Lang, one of four young men who formed Woodstock Ventures to produce the festival, "That's what means the most to me — the connection to one another felt by all of us who worked on the festival, all those who came to it, and the millions who couldn't be there but were touched by it."

By Wednesday 60,000 people had already arrived and set up camp. On Friday, the roads were so clogged with cars that performing artists had to arrive by helicopter. Though over 100,000 tickets were sold prior to the festival weekend, they became unnecessary as swarms of people descended on the concert grounds to take part in this historic and peaceful happening. Four days of music - half a million people - rain, and the rest is history.

Bali Ram made his way to the front of the stage after asking friends from Millbrook to tend his pottery booth. The stage was up to his chin. His long, thick black hair was down to his waist; his upper body was bare. He was wearing only his underwear.

Drunk out of his mind most of the time, Bali didn't take drugs at Woodstock. He said, "The first day Ravi Shankar was there and Joan Baez. Joan Baez's husband was in the jail at that time. Baez, in her 20's, was known for her anti-war songs.

It rained for three days. The first day's performances were shut down due to the heavy rainfall and winds. Bali said, "People crowded in the river. Most were naked. If the rain had not come, more people could have joined, but there was thunder and lightning."

According to Bali there were no fights, no violence, just a half a million people digging the music and most of them stoned or completely wacked out on drugs or booze. He stayed three days, and he recalls securing his pottery stand at night and going to Millbrook to spend the night during the festival. Bali said, "Every bush was burning with people making love and naked alongside the river." He saw them while he was cooling off in the river and claimed he was not one of those in the bushes. "People were necking and making love and no one cared. The whole village had gone mad and it was not just young people. They were old and young. Children. Boys and girls going around naked. The crowds were so thick I could not see from one end to the other." The people he knew in the village were involved in attending their shops during the festival. It was total chaos.

Portable latrines lined the perimeters but he noticed that most people went into the river to relieve themselves. Whether they were naked or clothed they didn't care. Many walked naked on the street. No one seemed to notice the nakedness as being unusual. In India in large marketplaces, he saw people naked. There is no law requiring clothing. They shop early in the morning before the flies bombard. He said he felt like he was back in India.

It took one week to clean up the garbage. Bali said that two people were killed because they were in sleeping bags when the tractor collecting garbage ran over them because nobody could see them. It was just an accident. One report indicated one person was killed in this incident.

Again, Bali Ram was part of a historic event that will be remembered for decades. He was 34 years old.

The Party's Over

Repeated FBI raids ended Leary's free ride at Millbrook. G. Gordon Liddy later became legendary for his criminal role in the Watergate break-in. Tommy and Billy Hitchcock served all those living at Millbrook eviction notices. Leary was at Berkeley and had "no intention of leaving the property and would have to be driven out at gun point" after four years of occupancy. Leary stated that, "Our response to the eviction order would determine the fate of the psychedelic movement not to mention world history for eons to come, the very stars in their courses, and so forth – and that we should defy that spoiled rich brat prick Tommy at the cost of our lives if necessary. Passive resistance. Dig caves in the hill, etc."

Greenfield summed Millbrook up in Leary's biography, stating, "During the years Tim Leary called Millbrook home, chaos was the rule rather than the exception. For those who had authentic peak experiences there, journeying out of their bodies to experience another reality, the estate was paradise on earth. For others, it was a vision of hell. With the lord of the manor now heading into yet another new direction, the moment in time that had been Millbrook was over."

Bali said that his group stayed after Leary and his followers were gone. Billy Hitchcock had donated $25,000 towards the purchase of an old dude ranch in Arizona, about 60 miles from Tucson. Druch mentioned that $45,000 came from "Seymour the

Messiah" and several people got jobs to help pay for the property that would become an ashram.

Bali, Haines, Druch, and 17 others left Millbrook in a caravan of three full sized U-Haul trucks, a couple battered old pickups, one with a goat, several vehicles, five dogs, two cats, and their property. It took five days to drive from New York to their new ashram.

The night before they left, Bali said that Billy invited them to dinner at the bungalow, and they departed Millbrook on good terms with the Hitchcock family.

Pottery for Goldwater

Susan, Leary's troubled daughter, lived for three weeks at the Arizona ashram. Rosemary, Leary's new wife, claimed that Haines got the Millbrook bell that he used in his ashram in Arizona.

"What about the bell, Bali?" I asked. "Did Haines take a bell from Millbrook?"

"Oh, my God! I almost forgot about that. Yes. It was like Liberty Bell, it was so huge. It took eight or ten men to move it onto the truck." I couldn't help giggling.

International performances had ended before Haines and Bali moved to Millbrook. Bali said he danced in every state at universities and colleges. New York had been his home in America. Bali had a performance in Arizona and people liked him very much and kept asking him to stay.

Arizona called to Bali, so after Woodstock, he put New York behind him and began his new life in Arizona with the other nineteen caravan members. Druch said that they arrived in May, 1968, but Bali is adamant that he attended Woodstock, and that he went back to Millbrook to sleep during the festival.

The property was ten miles off the main highway, and they felt that they would not be harassed by law enforcement, as they had encountered at Millbrook since Leary was not a part of this venture. Bali spoke to me as though the ranch belonged to him, but Druch indicated that the property was owned by a group of the residents, which Bali confirmed. Haines had fizzled out as an agent and Bali did his own bookings, performing around the U.S. at mostly colleges and universities.

Bali said that Haines lived in the guest house, while he occupied the main house. He said they also built additional housing for ashram visitors. Rather than livestock, they raised peacocks and exotic pigeons that he said looked like fancy chickens. Double tulips came from Netherlands and grapes hung from a pergola in the yard. On the 325 acres, he could stand on one side and couldn't see the other end. Valleys and meadows were on the property, with mountains nearby. Many people came to visit and stayed at the ranch while servants tended to their needs.

A movie was being filmed nearby and Bali and Haines heard that Greg Sierra was among the cast members. Haines went to the movie set, found his friend, and invited him to the ranch. Sierra told all the people on the set that if they got fed up they could go the ranch. Most of the actors and actresses on the set came to the ranch to relax for a few hours during breaks between shootings. Bali said they were still in costume with their makeup on. None of them stayed the night. Bali cannot remember their names. They wanted his picture and they toured the ranch and pottery shop. Since it was an ashram, there were meditation classes in session so they could have quiet time.

On the ranch, he made his own kiln and bought his potter's wheel in Phoenix, from a woman who owned a shop, and he bought two wheels and clay from her. She asked for his address, and she and her husband began delivering his supplies to the ranch. They said, "Bali, you don't have to go for your supplies. We love your ranch and we will come down and stay here and bring you the supplies." She had cancer and they would stay overnight on the ranch, which was a panacea for her. The lovely woman adored Bali, the ranch, his artwork, and offered to give him most of his supplies at no charge.

"No, don't do that," he would scold her.

"Bali, I'm your friend. I want you to succeed. I want you to make beautiful things like you always do." She was very kind, middle aged and her husband loved her very much. Bali said he used to cry just to see them together there was so much love between them.

In storage he has pictures of the kiln and potter's wheel showing him making his pottery. All of the designs were his own originals which he tweaked to the western country he was living in. At first he purchased glazes to make a color. A Native American woman friend, who was half Navaho and half Cherokee, showed him how to find *caliche* on his property which he used for clay. Bali said that her great grandfather came from India to build railroads and he married a Native American. *Caliche* was found in the tall, dry grasses under mesquite trees. He told me he had to be very careful because of the rattlesnakes in the grass. They would dig down about 18 inches and find a butter-like substance. *Caliche* is a sedimentary rock, a hardened deposit of calcium carbonate. This calcium carbonate cements together other materials, including gravel, sand, clay, and silt. When he put the hardpan in water it became beautiful clay. Grinding stones to make his own colors for glazes, he had everything that a potter should have.

There were washes like dry riverbeds, and when it rained in the desert, they would fill up so fast that he could hear the water coming like the roar of a tank. In the middle of night he could really hear it because it was so quiet. After these flash floods, he would dig for rocks and earthen materials.

Each piece of pottery was a work of art, and he enjoyed adding the road runner to the designs to represent the southwest.

Bali decided to sell his pottery sitting along the side of the highway, as he did in the village of Woodstock. He had purchased a vendor's license from City Hall for a day to test the waters. A highway patrolman was driving by and pulled over, thinking he had found a violation. The officer got out of the car and asked, "Do you have permission to sell all these beautiful things?"

"Thank you for sayings it's beautiful, but I do have a permit for a day. Today only."

"May I see it?" and Bali handed him the paperwork. "Okay, thank you." The patrolman looked over Bali's artwork and liked it very much because Bali had the design of a road runner on it and a line of quail with the chicks following their parents.

"How much are they?" he asked about a mug and plate.

"All together they are twenty-five dollars," and they completed the sale. Bali said he hated to charge him but he didn't want the officer to think he was trying to give him a bribe.

One day Bali packed up all the pottery he had on hand in a large suitcase and went to the mall in Scottsdale. Luckily, the owner, Barry Goldwater, a five-term U. S. Senator, was visiting his store that day, which was unusual. He called Bali into his office. Bali put his suitcase down and opened it up. Bali thought he had seen photos of Senator Goldwater, but he didn't know that he was the *real* one. He gave his card to Goldwater as the Senator sat down and went through everything in the suitcase over and over. He called another man to his office, an assistant or sales manager, and directed him to buy everything Bali Ram had offered.

In 1961 the Scottsdale Fashion Square was built as a 3-story open-air structure and was one of the ten most profitable shopping malls in the U. S., which included a Goldwater's department store. Goldwater's grandfather's Jewish family had founded Goldwater's, the largest department store in Phoenix. The family department stores made the Goldwater family comfortably wealthy. His father, Baron, died in 1930, and Barry took over the very successful business.

Goldwater was so curious after he saw his pottery in Scottsdale, that he wanted to see Bali's operation for himself, being a little skeptical. He didn't quite believe that Bali made his own pottery and his own glazes from natural stone and dirt. Bali said, "His mind was curious like an explorer."

Bali picked up the phone at 8 o'clock one morning, and it was Goldwater. "Are you going to be on the ranch or are you going somewhere?"

"No. I'm on the ranch."

"Okay. Are you going to be there today or not?"

"I'm here 24 hours a day."

Dressed in faded, blue jeans worn at the knees, dusty cowboy boots, and well-worn cowboy hat, Barry Goldwater drove an old, dented pickup truck to the ranch. He showed up about 2:30 in the afternoon from Phoenix, even though he never actually said he was coming. Bali didn't recognize him at all because he was in a raggedy pickup truck and dressed like a poor rancher.

"I brought my truck. Do you have the pottery? Do you have anything to sell?"

"Sure," Bali told him and he showed Goldwater his workshop on the ranch.

"I want them all." He didn't ask Bali's price. He just said, "Put them on the truck and give me the estimate."

Goldwater bought every single piece for his Scottsdale store. Inside the department store, a special room encased in glass, was set up to display Bali's pottery, a room which Bali described as "like a palace." For the grand opening of the pottery showcase, he gave Bali a beautiful write up in the newspaper and Bali was invited to demonstrate his craft. For that one day, Bali was making pottery, trimming and coloring them. People lined up "like for a movie ticket" all around his glass room. Some waved, some spoke but Bali couldn't hear because he was on the other side of the glass.

Once a month Goldwater would return driving himself to the ranch, in what Bali called his disguise, in his raggedy pickup truck and worn-out blue jeans to buy all of Bali's work, even the rejects. Rejects sold for $60, a good price at that time.

An Indian Soul in a Western Body

Desmond Doig sketching

Calcutta's name changed to "Kolkuta" in 2001. It was always called "the city of joy." Doig resided in Calcutta many years, and published two books of his sketches with descriptions and the history of historical buildings, temples, monuments, etc. One is, *Calcutta: An Artist's Impression*, which is in black and white and began first as an article in *The Statesman*, the Calcutta newspaper, in June of 1966 and resulted in 75 weekly installments giving a portrait of the city before being complied into a book.

Doig's Sketch of Raj Bhavan, Calcutta

Another example of his lovely water-colors, and black and white sketches is called *My Kind of Kathmandu*. Both books give intimate details and biography of both cities, described in his exquisite style of prose.

Hours of research about Doig's personal life has resulted in dead ends. I emailed *The Statesman* with no response. Bali told me that I will not get a response. Many times, as a reporter, he would investigate and do an exposé on sensitive, even dangerous issues. Often, Bali said, a reporter's name was fictitious and the newspaper closely protected the correspondents. Doig only mentioned "wife" once in all the material I have read that he authored. No wife's first name, no mention of children. Bali said he was protecting his family.

Doig had many talents. Among them was his skill at architectural design. Inspired by James Hilton's novel, *The Lost Horizon*, he was driven to bring to life great designs for a hotel being constructed in Kathmandu, Nepal, which was named *Shangri La*. He was guided by the imagery of Hilton and his own passion and adoration for Nepal and the Himalayas. Although Shangri La was a fictional place in the novel, his vision helped to create a beautiful, harmonious, and serene retreat with gardens that are a paradise. The spacious and elegant lounge includes a library and easy chairs with side tables allowing patrons to do two of Doig's favorites pastimes: enjoy reading while having a stiff drink.

Desmond Doig Library & Lounge
in Shangri-La Hotel, Kathmandu, Nepal

Occasionally, Bali told me, Doig became depressed and reclusive. He would go into seclusion to re-group. He was sensitive and generous. Doig brought joy and respect to all those around him. There was a constant flow of visitors who dropped by for tea or for a meal. Doig, the grandest of hosts, took them around Calcutta to sight-see, always taking his sketch pad. Everywhere he went he sketched.

Doig found a way to make people shine. He helped individuals, such as Bali, his protégée, to enhance their natural gifts. Doig helped many families in need and he used his influence to assist people in finding jobs. He arranged children to be sent to school whose parents could not afford the education. Caring and considerate, he always saw the potential in people.

"I admire him and love him. I miss him very much, every day," Bali said with his voice cracking from sweet memories. There were times when Bali was young and Doig's guidance was a nuisance. Bali would think to himself, "Who the hell does this guy think he is. He's not my father," as Doig groomed him in etiquette, manners, and the proper way to address diplomats and dignitaries. "You have no manners," he would say to Bali, or, "You should behave yourself." He was strict with Bali, and it upset the young boy. Bali used to cry and wondered why the man just wouldn't shut up.

"Just watch yourself and be aware who you are dealing with," Doig would caution. Of course, Bali realized when he was admonished it was all training and life lessons to prepare him for his future.

Doig's dream was that Bali would be able to earn a living and live a successful life. "I was smelly, dirty, with torn clothes, but Desmond saw something in me when I was a kid in the park in Calcutta," Bali told me. "Desmond always saw the potential of people and he wanted help them to be higher than himself. He had no ego."

"I'm not going to live forever, Bali," Desmond said as he sat across the table from Bali when he was a teenager. "Bali, look at me!" Bali said that out of respect, per the custom of his country, he wouldn't look into his eyes. "Look at me. I will die one day and you must be able to do things for yourself. You have to work hard. When I die, we'll meet again, forever and ever." Bali faithfully obeyed him and practiced dancing eight hours a day.

Many artists knew Doig and came to entertain him when he threw cocktail parties. Bali loved seeing the different dances performed, including cabaret style. Doig lived in a very "high-class mansion," according to Bali, and on the roof it was like a theater with a wall waist high and a marble floor. There were carpets, pillows, flowers, and plants. The roof was nicely decorated like a stage. Bali described Doig "like a maharaja, people came to perform for him."

Doig would tap on the table while people were eating and would say, "Ladies and gentlemen, I have someone I wish to introduce you to, an artist, Bali Ram." Bali said that different people would drop by "every half hour to see Doig including princes and princesses. Nehru visited and his sister fell in love with Desmond." On Saturdays and Sundays Doig would take his sketch book, colored pencils, and pack sandwiches, and went to filthy areas where no other reporter would venture in order to capture the essence of the poverty-stricken people of India, capturing how the beggars, the poor, and the sick people lived.

Doig's book, *Mother Teresa: Her people and Her Work* brought world-wide recognition to her. Bali has pictures of himself with Doig and Mother Teresa. The photos are in India but he said he is unable to get them. "Well, Bali," I asked him, "India is very progressive and technical; can't they just scan them and send them to me by email?"

"Not where they are, Terrie. A friend has them in a little village. There is not even a post office. They have not even electricity. They light their houses by rendering fat from their goats – still today."

Doig's wife and children stayed in New York most of the time. It was only during the winter months of November and December that the mosquitoes were dormant. There were three things for a mother to fear: mosquitoes, flies and deadly snakes - especially cobras. Encephalitis was a horrible disease that mosquitoes brought to humans. Bali said that, since we were adults, he would speak frankly with me and that it can make a man's testicles swell so terrifically that he could not walk and would have to be carried by friends or in a wheelbarrow.

Cobras grew to 17 feet long and one reason was their uncanny ability to find a cow with a full utter. He said the cobra would wrap his body around her back legs and pull them together so she could not move. The snake then would suckle on the teats without biting the cow. Then when it was full of milk the cobra would have to leave quickly, for the bovine would go after it to trample it. One evening at this house in New Delhi, Bali was about to retire for the night. His bed was on a screened porch near his garden. He noticed that the sheets were puffed a little. He pulled back the sheets to be greeted by a cobra. Bali was very frightened but was clever enough to go to the kitchen. He poured milk into a bowl, put it in the garden, the snake followed the scent, and slithered from Bali's bed to the garden to drink the milk on the grass. Bali did not sleep in that bed for a very long time.

Many people notice cobras in their houses, gliding behind the couch, or along the wall, but mostly, where the villages have thatched or bamboo roofs, the snakes are on the roofs. Mice make nests in the natural roofing material and the cobras go after the mice. Bali said most often the snakes are not aggressive toward the families.

Doig's brother, Stanley, was a colonel in the army and rented a house in New Delhi. Many people visited his garden because he developed a rose tree. Visitors and friends would stroll through the garden and sit outside for tea. Bali remembered him washing his hands after he had gardened in order to pick up Bali, a small boy at the time, and twirl him around.

"I am so happy that America has recognized you as a dancer and a great artist," he told Bali. Doig received letters from people from all over the world informing him of Bali's success. He was so proud of Bali Ram. He would also read about Bali in newspapers. "I am very proud of you. You have never let my hopes for you down. You shine like a star."

Doig visited Bali twice in New York when Bali was living there, not including the Yeti scalp incident. Bali was concerned that his dear friend had gained weight. Bali has always been disciplined with his own diet. Doig loved to sit and read.

"Come on. Let's go walking," Bali urged Doig. "We'll go to a museum and talk while we walk." The extra weight, Bali felt, contributed to his fatal heart attack in 1989.

Doig left India in favor of Nepal in the 1980s. He said, "Bali Ram, I want to make my home in Nepal.

I just love the Nepalese people. My soul belongs to them. If you come to visit me, you will find me in Nepal. Come to Nepal. It will be home to you." Those were his last words to Bali.

The Loss of Desmond Doig

(Found on-line with no source indicated)
October 14, 1983
By A Staff Reporter

Desmond Doig, the noted British journalist, writer and artist died in Bir Hospital Thursday noon after a massive heart attack. He was 63.

Mr. Doig, who served with the 5th Royal Gurkha Rifles and saw action at Monte Cassino during the Second World War, had been living in Kathmandu for the past twelve years.

Brian Brake: Photographer & Friend

"Bali, this is great. This is what I need from you," I told him while proofing the book, as he proceeded to feed me more yummy tidbits about his experiences. When his copy of the proof came back to me, Bali added photographers' names to some captions. Two photographs were taken by Brian Brake, New Zealand's most renowned international photographer. Brake joined the National Film Unit as a cameraman. *Snows of Aorangi*, one of the films he directed, was the first New Zealand film nominated for an Academy Award in the Best Short Subject category in 1959. He moved to London and was a freelance photographer in Europe, Africa, and Asia until the mid 1960's when he began working for *Life* magazine exclusively.

Brake, Doig, and Bali were close friends. He was an advisor to Doig on photography, angles, and lighting. "He was a beautiful artist and a sweetheart of a person. We would party at Desmond's house in Calcutta until four or five in the morning. I was sleeping on the roof and Brian woke me up early in the morning because he wanted to take my pictures while the sun was just coming out, in the right light," Bali remembered how Brake played with light for his photos.

Brake loved Bali's cooking, and after exhausting photo sessions, he would come into the living room, sit on the couch and say, "Bali, I'm hungry. Do you have something to eat? Give me some of your curry."

While Bali was performing in London, he was staying at Brake's house with his roommate who called

Brake to inform him that Bali was in London. Brake flew home from India to see his performance. Bali said that Brake never missed a performance if he was in the region, including Bombay, Madras, Pondicherry in India, and Cambodia and Thailand. Bali said that Brake loved to film and take photos in the rain. Most of his work is displayed at the Museum of New Zealand *Te Papa Tongarewa.* In 1998 the museum featured *Monsoon: Brian Brake's Images of India.* He was careful to retain his negatives and transparencies; however, he gave Bali the negatives to the photos that are in this book. Bali asked if I was able to contact Brake. "He will be thrilled that you are doing my story." I broke the news to Bali that Brake died at the age of 61, a year before Desmond passed. He had lost another dear friend.

Bali remembered Brake "sitting in shit for hours" just to get the right shot.

Brian Brake on location

Brian Brake

Haines is Gone

Bali and Haines bought property in Southern California near Hemet. It was 1986, and after seventeen years at the ranch, the guests and residents had dwindled along with their hopes of a thriving ashram, so they sold it. Bali, Haines, along with their two Lhasa Apsos named Tashi and Tara, and their cat, loaded into their truck for the long drive ahead. There was a small caravan of two pickup trucks and a couple of cars accompanying Haines and Bali made up of people from the ranch to help them move. There was a mobile home on the property where they were going to stay until they built a house.

They had just arrived from Arizona about 3:30 a.m., totally exhausted from the July heat crossing Death Valley. They piled out of the vehicles too tired to bring the luggage into the scantily furnished mobile home. Haines took a shower and Bali went to a bedroom while one couple slept in the living room. They did not even say good night to each other as they hit their beds and fell asleep.

Bali usually got up very early to check on Haines because of his diabetes. He made tea and opened the door of the bedroom and Tashi wedged his way past Bali. Bali noticed Haines wasn't moving his toes when he opened the door and he said, "Wow, that's weird." He always saw Haines's big toe sticking out of the covers and it always wiggled. The cat was sitting under Haine's arm, and his dog had been sitting next to the cat on the floor.

"Bill! Bill! Bill! What the hell? Did he drop some ink on him?" he asked himself because his body was purple. Bali checked his friend. Haines was dead.

He woke up the other two and said, "Hey, Bill Haines is gone."

"Where did he go?"

"No, he's gone. He's dead." They both jumped up and Bali called the police and fire department. Bali told me, "He had a big hole in his heart. His heart bust open."

The fact that they didn't talk because they were both so exhausted nor did they say good night to each other still bothers Bali. He never got to say goodbye to his friend and companion.

The ambulance came. Haines had shed all his clothes when he went to bed due to the heat, and Bali recalled, choking up, "They put him in a plastic bag like they were taking him to the dumpster." They put him on ice in a body bag to preserve his body until they did an autopsy.

Bali called Haines's mother Margaret who lived in St. David, Arizona, and she flew out and made the funeral arrangements. He said he forgot his own sorrow when he looked at Haines's mother with her tears streaming down her face. She called her sister in California and her sister came right away. Both Bali and Haines's mother felt better because they were not alone. She had his body transferred home.

In the same week, Bali went back to India. The sorrow and loss of his friend and manager of his life for 25 years hit him and he broke down in grief. In spite the fact that they argued and Haines was controlling and a pain in the ass at times, Bali said, "Well, I guess you can say we stayed together, how you say? 'til death do us part." Bali returned to Arizona to attend college.

Bali Falls in Love

Blue eyed, champagne blonde, lovely, and a very bright mathematician, Amy was a tutor at Pima Community College. Bali was taking classes at the university in Tucson and a teacher told him that he would have to go see the tutor assigned to him. They gave Bali her room number, and he said that as he walked in, she dropped her pencil and paper at the sight of him. He picked up the things she dropped and he asked what happened.

"Oh, I don't know. They just slipped out of my hand," Amy said. He was drop-dead gorgeous and also very shy.

Amy began to tutor Bali and, what seemed to him very early in their association, she informed him, "My mom and dad would like to meet you." So he went with her to her parents' house for dinner. Her father, Eugene Stagner, was a retired Navy officer and served aboard a ship during Vietnam. After the dinner was finished, still sitting around the table, her dad asked him questions like, "Do you have a girlfriend?" and, "Do you intend to marry some day?" Bali said that her father was "feeling me out" and that he was so naïve at the time he didn't get the implication. Bali wasn't aware how much Amy liked Bali.

"No. I don't have any plans to marry nor do I have anybody special in my life."

"Don't you want to someday?" her father asked.

"Yeah. It's okay. But I don't run after women," Bali responded and they all laughed. He said Amy was nudging him under the table as her father questioned Bali.

Every week or two her parents invited him to dinner. Amy was coming to visit more and more often to see him and take him places. They went to the movies. They went swimming. They strolled through lovely gardens. They were good companions, but he thought of her as a friend. He was not physically attracted to this lovely blond young lady, 30 years his junior. She was attracted to Bali but he didn't realize it until one day they were dancing together and he said, "It happened." All this time he was so naïve, and then, with the embrace during their dance, a courtship began.

Bali told me, "I told her everything and I said I'm a dancer and I have to go out performing and things, and she said, 'No no no. I like you very much and don't worry about it.'" He did U.S. tours from Arizona.

They married and had two children together. Andrew Bali Ram was born first and then four years later came their daughter, Shamina. Bali was very content and this was the first and only woman he had loved enough to marry. After they were married she was still a tutor, and later became a tenth grade math teacher. Bali must have been about 53 and she was 20 when they met. Bali said Amy was 22 when he married her.

They were both still going to school when they had children. He went in the afternoon and she attended at night. It was very hard for her with kids and going to school. Bali was mostly the caregiver, cooking and tending to them when they were sick. They were both very good parents. Then he said that something happened and he had no idea what turned things against him. The marriage began to crumble and Bali thought that when she became employed as a teacher that her friends might have influenced her against Bali.

They were together until Andrew was eleven (Andrew says he was nine). When she left Bali she moved in with her parents for a year or two. Bali offered a parenting plan, "Look, Amy, the kids they stay six months with you, six months with me."

Bali's Children, Shamina & Andrew, apx. ages 7 & 9

She said yes, and they both offered support for the children. When I met Bali at age 76, he was still paying child support for his daughter, on a small, part-time income. He had not invested his money when he was earning the big bucks performing, and had no residual income from the ranch. In September of 2012, Shamina turned eighteen. Bali said it had been ten years since she had talked with him.

Andrew and he remained very close and Bali loved Amy's parents and said that they were very kind to him after the marriage dissolved.

Bali worked at the Radisson Suites in Tucson after they split up. He said he was the manager at the time that Janet Napolitano was Governor, and Bali was her server when she came to the hotel. That was the only time he served anyone in his position as manager.

Shala Mattingly had lost track of Bali just before he and Haines went to Millbrook. She said she was on-line and found a reference to a man named Bali Ram teaching in a dance studio in Arizona. She was able to contact him and restore their friendship after twenty-five years.

"My children! I will show you a picture one of these days. Look like Kashmir people. Beautiful, beautiful faces. My daughter absolutely look like Italian. Very beautiful. Ummm," he sighed, thinking of his beloved children.

Amy remarried and currently lives in Florida with Shamina. Andrew is attending college in Florida and lives with his fiancée, Emily.

Bali's son, Andrew and his fiancée, Emily 2013

Andrew's Life with Father

W hen I called Bali's son, Andrew, I explained that Daniel, my son, and his dad had been roommates in Bend, Oregon, for a while. They were both working at the same restaurant and pub. Daniel was captivated with Bali's story and kept prompting me to meet Bali and listen to his remarkable life since I was writing novels based on true events.

Andrew said when he visited his dad in Bend, Bali told him that he wanted his story to be told to others. He was very passionate about it. I told Andrew that his father's life was astonishing and that I didn't have a good time line on many events. Bali is used to telling short versions of his stories – one- liners – about each incident, and I was pursuing the details to chronicle his life.

"I heard most of dad's stories for the first time when I went out to see him. When we were getting off the plane and I saw him in the terminal it was kind of like looking at a hermit and not the fact that he was old, but he had just aged more than I had expected." It had been ten years since Andrew had seen his father. That first night that Andrew was in Bend with his fiancée Emily, he said he felt guilty that he hadn't seen him in so long. For a young struggling student, the cost of a plane flight and going across country was difficult for him, and since his mom is living on a teacher's salary, she was not able to help either. Andrew was emotionally torn, and the first night it was really hard for him with his dad. After that, he said he enjoyed the trip and said it was very nice. They stayed for five days. He has his own place with Emily, living the sparse life of college students.

Andrew was twenty years old when I interviewed him on the phone and he had visited his father in fall of 2011. He said, "I was nine when my parents divorced. My mom had her story, and he had his. But I never saw him perform his dancing, so when I finally saw him dance in Bend, it was miraculous. I was shocked and amazed. It was the last day that we were there, and we were sitting in this auditorium, and he was walking around the auditorium and he was stumbling, because he's older (76 at the time) and he lost his footing. Well, on stage it was like he's 17 or 20 again. He was gliding on stage and I was very moved."

I asked Andrew, "Were you aware of his background when you were together as a family?"

Bali was in his mid fifties when Andrew was born and his glory days of dancing around the world and in New York were behind him.

"I feel guilty. One picture I saw, he performed with Miss Universe 1954, I think, (actually Miss India 1952) and then I saw that picture as a little kid," referring to the photo Bali has at approximately age seven on the seashore with Gandhi. "He's always had the picture, and I distinctly remember it, so when I saw it in a text book, I said, wow, this is incredible because I was a little kid, and I thought, oh he's making up stories. It was pretty fascinating. But how he got discovered, that was probably the coolest story out of all of them," referring to his serendipitous encounter with Doig.

Bend reminds Bali of Katmandu. The river running through it, the mountains surrounding it, the shape of the mountains, the climate, were so much like his homeland. Andrew recognized the similarities between Bend and Kathmandu. He said there was a desert right at the base of the Himalayas in Kathmandu and then rising to 29,000 feet, is the top of Mount Everest. "It's kind of funny because Mt. Bachelor is right there in Bend, and you have that as the pinnacle in town."

Andrew was attending the University of Central Florida studying aerospace engineering. His goal was to work at NASA and get to Mars, but since the national budget has cut so much of the space exploration, he is gearing for the Department of Defense or for a private company. When I first talked with Andrew, he was a junior (2012), with a minor in business because he wishes to move up quickly into a managerial position where he can run projects, and be in charge of building new technology from the ground up. His goal is to be an engineer for a new fighter jet or a missile design.

"A lot of things nowadays that we take for granted, engineers have made." He said he has a different concept of the world after taking some of his classes. Now when he looks at a car or a crane he will never view it as just another car or just another crane. They are really fetes of engineering and design. He said it was just his "nerdiness" talking, but even a bridge or a jet flying makes him stop and ponder about the engineering that went into the design.

"I tell Emily about it and she just shakes her head and nods. I am very passionate about it. If you love what you do from the beginning that is part of the bliss in life."

Andrew's mother, Amy, re-married, but is single now. No more children. Just his sister and him. Shamina hasn't stayed close to her dad. He said that she is a typical teenager. He said, "I've tried to warm her up to the idea of talking with Dad but she wants nothing to do with him. She's 17 and she wants to do what 17 year old girls are doing, and not worry about other things, so I think she'll warm up to the idea of contacting him because he is getting older."

Andrew's voice changed to mirth when I asked him about his favorites memories of his father when the family was together. He remembered something he enjoyed very much. They lived in a townhouse, and his father would walk Shamina and him to school. At the time Andrew was learning his multiplication tables and his father would quiz Andrew on the way to school. He said it was how he got started in his love of math. Even though his mother was a math teacher, his dad got the ball rolling and it came so easily for Andrew because his father was testing him every day. "That was every single day."

He remembered that they had neighbors down the road who had Doberman Pinchers, and his dad would always make jokes about them and would make him laugh. His dad would say, "Be quiet", or "Shut up" to the dogs, and it was in such a funny way that Andrew would break out laughing.

He also remembered in kindergarten they would have Play-Doh and Bali would act out stuff. One time Andrew had just watched *Snow White* and made a really bad looking apple out of Play-Doh, and his father pretended to eat it and played dead for what seemed like ten minutes. He said to a five year old, a few minutes seemed like an hour, and he went around frantically thinking he killed his dad. Finally, Bali got up and had to comfort his sobbing child.

Bali always encouraged his son to dance and sing. Andrew said he was obsessed with dinosaurs and while his dad was behind the camera taking movies, Andrew would dance to *Triceratops Rock*. Andrew still has those films.

Andrew also loves to cook and knew he got that quality from his father.

One of his favorite memories was when his father took him to a holy festival, a harvest festival of colors. They went to a park and the kids, running around in bathing suits, put food coloring in squirt guns or super soakers and dowsed people with the colorful sprays. What fun!

Andrew said that Tucson had the largest concentration of Native Americans and Nepalese people in one location, "and they were all squirting each other." Everyone was eating and enjoying having fun. He said it was like an Indian Thanksgiving, except it was a lot messier.

One other thing he remembered: "I don't know if this was a happy memory, maybe more reassuring. Every morning his father would get up around four a.m., kneel on a rug he placed on the floor, and had a special cup in which he burned incense, and he quietly observed his father in prayer. At that time Andrew said that his father was still Hindu during the time that his parents were married, but he thought that he had converted to Christianity. When Andrew first went to college, he took a world religion class. He asked his teacher if that practice was Muslim, and his teacher said that Hindus can also pray like that at times. When he went to visit his dad in Bend, Bali still had the glass cup. It brought a smile to his face recalling sweet memories of his life with his father.

"Bali," I asked him during a phone call, "one of things that Andrew remembers about you is that you would get up early in the morning and put down a rug in the Hindu tradition. After you were baptized as a Catholic with Mother Teresa, did you still practice Hinduism?"

"Yeah. It's in me. Just to respect to my country. I used to sit on a rug and light the candle or oil lamp. I still do it. It is very soothing to look at the oil lamp in the living room and have some rose petals all around it. It is very beautiful."

"Do you go to Catholic church?"

"I do. Catholic church is right next to my work."

"Andrew said it was such a fond memory of his watching you on the rug. Do you meditate or do you pray?"

Bali said, "I pray. I meditate. Not much difference between praying and meditation."

"How long do you do it each morning?"

"At least I do for fifteen minutes, maybe twenty minutes. After I bathe, I sit, I light the lamp, and I meditate. If I have the cross, I put the candle on. It's ritual that is bred into me. I just can't help it."

"I think it's wonderful," I told him.

"Whether I have money or job or not, I never forget that. Always. You know I was penniless for long, long time, but I never forget praying. Yeah. When Andrew and Shamina were little kids, they used to come into bedroom when I praying or meditating."

"Andrew said you still have that cup, too."

"Yes." And he paused. "Mother Teresa was very helpful. Of course, she always wanted to talk about Jesus, you know. But when she saw me sitting down meditating, she appreciate that. She said, 'All the praying goes to God no matter who you are or what you are doing. We are all branches of one tree.' That's what she said, her exact words, 'We are all branches of one tree, but all the roots, all the way into the ground, are one.' So I like that very, very much."

Neither Andrew nor his mother met Bali's parents. Bali told him that they both lived to be over 100 years old.

Andrew said that his mother Amy probably would not want to talk with me about Bali. He said that she really wouldn't talk about his dad to him. He thought that Bali being foreign was hard on his grandparents, but they warmed up to it and they liked him and, of course, they love Andrew and his sister. "Mom just doesn't talk about him."

Andrew remembered that his parents would argue when he was a kid and he thought the main thing was that his dad would take care of them while his mother had to work. Money was tight and even though Bali looked for work, he was unemployed most of the time, and Andrew felt that strained the relationship for those years. Finally, his mom said that she couldn't do it anymore. Her decision to divorce had not really been discussed. His mother told Andrew and Shamina that their father was very loving and caring, but it was just that they were not compatible. Andrew said the greatest thing that his mother is thankful for is that they conceived his sister and him.

When they told Andrew about the breakup, Andrew took it very hard, but his dad was calm and said that they were both making the best of the situation. Andrew remembered that he was in their bedroom when they broke the shocking news to him. As soon as they told him, Andrew went to the bathroom and locked himself inside. He was very upset. His mom and dad tried to talk him out of there, but he stayed in the bathroom for about three hours. He said he was pretty young and it was very difficult for him to cope with his family being torn apart.

Looking back on it, he said now he doesn't regret it because the experience made him the person that he is today. And then meeting his dad later in life has brought him a greater appreciation for who he is and where he comes from. Seeing his dad inspires him. He would like to go to India and Nepal to see where his ancestors have been and how they have lived. In the last twenty years, India is finally catching up with the rest of the world, and it hadn't really been changed much before then in the years that people have been on this planet. Emily, his fiancé, and he plan to go there in the next five years.

I told Andrew about the Shangri La Hotel in Kathmandu with a thirteen minute tour on line which attributed much of the design to Desmond Doig and features the bar dedicated to Doig.

Emily's background is Scottish-American and she is first generation American. Her mother is from Scotland, and in Scotland they have a Buddhist Temple called the *Kugu Samye Ling*. Many celebrities like Tom Cruise have gone there for a spiritual retreat. Emily visited the temple and the Tibetan monks dress in the red garbs.

Andrews said his mother converted to Buddhism in honor of his father's country, even though Bali was

Hindu and converted to Catholic. A lot of the pictures when she was younger showed that she really embraced the culture. He said she has *saris* and she still eats curry to this day. He said Shamina embraces the culture, also, even though she wouldn't admit it. She wears *dikas* which is the dot that goes on a woman's forehead. She also wears bangles given to her by her father which are about twenty bracelets that go on an arm. Whether they like to admit it or not, he is still a part of their lives.

Andrew has called his father for various recipes that his mother wanted. His mother said, "You know, if it weren't for everything else, I would want your father around for his cooking. He was one hell of a cook." Andrew remembered that Bali had made a delicious Nepalese tea for them when they lived together. Emily wanted the recipe, which I got from Bali and sent to them. Andrew, like Bali, loves to cook and he said he prepares their meals almost every day, including Indian recipes which Emily enjoys, also. She is vegetarian and Andrew said it makes it easier to please her because a lot the Indian dishes are vegan. He said he's a carnivore himself, so he normally puts some kind of meat in the dishes, especially chicken. He loves chicken.

To illustrate his father's humor, while visiting Bali in Bend, Emily asked him why he eats beef. She knows that in India cows are sacred. Bali said, "Well, I only eat beef here because it is an American cow. It is not a Nepalese cow. It's not sacred." Andrew said they laughed. He said his father comes up with these jokes and has a great sense of humor.

Andrew asked me what things I know about his father because he's Googled Bali. He said he didn't know his father lived at 30 Rock before until he saw the newspaper clippings. He thought that John D.

Rockefeller III gave him his own apartment to live in and his own cooking show in the '60's. I confirmed that he held cooking classes through the Asia Society (Rockefeller may have had a hand in setting up the classes) and that prominent men came to the show and took lessons from him. He *was* in an apartment, but Bali assured me it was *not* at 30 Rock, as Andrew had remembered. I told Andrew that I have a full page copy from the New York Times in 1965 featuring Bali, his cooking show and recipes.

Andrew said that it is hard for him wrap his mind around the fact that his father is going on 80 years old. I told him that I've done the math on a lot of things trying to figure out how old Bali was when events occurred or going backward from an approximate date to see how old he was because Bali seems to have no concept of time or dates. For instance, if the picture Bali has with Gandhi was taken when Bali was seven years old, it would have been around 1942. Bali told Mattingly years ago when he showed her the photo, that his mother was visiting Gandhi's ashram. Gandhi took brisk walks everyday of his life, and Bali chased him down when Gandhi was strolling on a beach, much to his mother's chagrin.

Andrew said he wishes he could just ask the people directly, but unfortunately most of the people have already died including Picasso, Marilyn Monroe, Kennedy, Gandhi, Mother Teresa, Martin Luther King, and Rockefeller.

Andrew said, "Wow. This is crazy. My father was a rock star in the 60's." He said his father fell into a decent niche in society when he came to America because of his dancing in India. He said that his dad was very fortunate and that he got his American dream, and although now it is not as illustrious as it was in the 60's, he feels that his father is very grateful and wants to share his story with others that these things are possible.

I told Andrew, "There is a small amount of "creative non-fiction" in some narrative. Even where he works, people think he's full of shit. They don't believe him and they don't give him respect. They don't want to listen to him. I feel that this book based on his life is going to give credibility to his life's work and his life's dignity."

"Yeah, I know," Andrew responded. "I hope that will happen to my mom."

Bali has flyers, and photos and his detailed memory of events. For instance, in the poor quality newspaper photo of Bali performing at the United Nations, it was clear that President Kennedy and Jacqueline were sitting in the front row. The prince and king in Sikkim were in Bali's photos with him.

Andrew said that in India and Nepal, he knows that stories are highly valued.

I told him I was going to see his father dance in March (2012) in Bend. Andrew said to be sure to observe him before and after the performance. He had watched him, and before Bali danced, he said his dad seemed to walk like an older man. When he got on stage he was transformed! It was like his father was enlightened. He saw his father do some leaps and said he was very graceful. Since a recorder was not allowed at the performance, I purchased the DVD of the dance program. Bali Ram opened the show and closed the show. I thought he was wonderful!

Andrew was so respectful and courteous and very intelligent. We had set up a time to talk by phone and on that day he called to let me know that that time would not work for him and we rescheduled the phone interview. Both of his parents and his grandparents must be very proud of this fine young man.

Bali Finds Bend, Oregon, U.S.A.

Walter, a friend who Bali grew up with in New York, had been in the Navy in the Vietnam war and had married a girl from that country. He had four brothers and two sisters, and they all loved Bali dearly. Walter called Bali one day and teasingly asked, "Guess what?"

"What?" Bali asked.

"Guess what happened to me?"

"What?" Bali knew he had been married for several years, "Did you get divorced?"

Walter laughed "No. I have good news."

"Well, you must have a new girlfriend."

"No, Bali," he laughed. "Don't make me feel like I am a bad guy."

Bali said, "No, you know people do this," and he paused. "Okay, maybe you won the lottery."

Walter said, "I wish. No. I am telling you that I have sent you a round trip ticket from Arizona to come to see my family. I'm a father."

Bali said he fell out of his chair with astonishment. "I don't believe it. Don't joke with me." It was his first child. Bali headed to Portland, Oregon, U.S.A., and after two weeks Bali was bored. Walter realized how dreary it was for Bali to be sitting in his house while he and his wife worked. Bali just looked out the window at the rain which seemed to go on day and night.

"Have you seen Bend?" Walter asked him.

"No. What is it?" Bali asked.

"Oh, it's a lovely town in the center of Oregon. It's very beautiful. You would like it. If you are going back to Arizona or New York, go by way of Bend and see the sights and then continue your trip."

As the bus left Portland, Bali could see blue skies and waterfalls. No rain. As he got closer to Bend, it was high desert with the Cascade Mountains looming in the distance, capped with snow. Arriving at the bus station, he went to a park and saw the river. The people living there seemed very happy and friendly. Bali decided to give it a try, and has resided in Bend since 2004, moving there at age 69.

The similarities between Bend and Nepal, is why he settled there. The climate is also similar to his village of Patan. One major difference is the quality of the water in the rivers between Bend and Nepal and India. Author Barbara Scott, in her book *Violet Shyness of their Eyes: Notes from Nepal,* described the water as such: "Kathmandu has some of the dirtiest water in the world. From one sip the following effects are possible in one to ninety days: salmonella, toxiogenic ecola, shigella, giardia, amoebas, worms, and hepatitis."

Nepal

Broken Top, Cascade Range, near Bend, Oregon. U.S.A.
Photo by Daniel Biggs, Jr.

Bali said about India, "Holy Ganges, that's the Ganges. In India, if you dip in the Ganges you go straight to heaven. It is so much polluted, you have no idea. I mean, there're dead bodies floating on it but it's the holiest if you don't care about that and just make a dip of it, you'll go to heaven. The men and women bathe in the same place sometime naked, sometime with clothes on. Doesn't matter. It's freezing cold coming from Mt. Everest, that water. It's ice cold. If you bathe in that river, I mean we are all adults, so I can say that your penis gets little because it's so cold."

Bend is the principal city of central Oregon and was the fastest growing city in Oregon until the crash of 2008 and its economy is recovering at this writing. Bend is located on the eastern edge of the Cascade Range, along the Deschutes River. The River runs through the heart of the city with well-traveled hiking and walking trails lining the river. There is a hillside of rocks between Daniel's house the Mill District that is a sanctuary for rock chucks. Daniel says they have their own Facebook page.

Ponderosa Pine forest transitions into the high desert, characterized by arid land, junipers, sagebrush, and bitter-brush. Daniel is an avid fly fisherman and is intimate with the thirteen Cascade lakes. His website is Bendflyfishing.com. Bend started as a logging town but is now identified as a gateway for many outdoor sports, including mountain biking, fishing, hiking, camping, rock climbing, white-water rafting, skiing, and golf. I add to that, a haven of micro breweries, a paradise for the serious beer connoisseur.

Personally, my husband Dan and I love to experience the restaurants in Bend, if I can pry Dan away from ribs at Baldy's. I suppose we are easy to please when we aren't the ones doing the preparation. La Grande is small and our family considers our house as the best dining in town.   Our sons always complimented us after each meal as we sat together at the dining room table. "Why would we bother to spend all of this time preparing a meal that tastes awful?" was my response after thanking them for their good manners. When they left home, I sent both of them off with our recipes in a binder I named, "Words of Wisdom and Culinary Delights." It contains my favorite words of wisdom including the poem, *If*, by Rudyard Kipling, and Robert Fulgrums' *All I Really Need to Know I Learned in Kindergarten.*

Healthy Living & More Recipes

Lessons 101 from Bali Ram for Indian cuisine: "Always use stems when using cilantro. In India your dish would not be accepted. The stems are where the vitamins and flavors are found.

"Never peel the ginger root (who knew?). Again, in India dish would be thrown out if skin cut off of ginger.

"Yogurt goes in pork or chicken curry dishes, not in lamb or beef. Pork is greasy and yogurt balances it out."

On his 17th birthday he went with Doig to celebrate and had pork and shrimp. He found he had an allergic reaction (most likely to the shrimp, as I do with undercooked shellfish). He began itching within five minutes and "swelled up." Therefore, he doesn't eat either. He does eat meat sparingly.

"Bali, tell me what your typical daily diet is like," I asked him.

Dried fruits such as pears, dates and figs serve to enhance his morning oatmeal along with pistachios or almonds. The oats are cooked with 1% milk and the dried fruit goes in with the oats. Once a week for breakfast he may have an omelet with vegetables such as peppers and spinach, but only egg whites. Never egg yolk. I have my own lifetime theory on the bad rap eggs have been given. The lecithin in the whites counteracts the cholesterol in yolks. A perfectly balanced food.

His second and final meal of the day is around three or four o'clock. He said he eats mostly beans and lentils.   Indian lentils are very nutritious.   Lots of vegetables especially dark green such as mustard greens and turnip greens grace his table.   Turnip greens, he claims, are good for the stomach giving a good bowel movement.   He chops onion and garlic, and browns them with ground pork or beef, then adds the greens and lets them cook another 15 or 20 minutes, adding a little water if needed.

Only "pure" wheat flour, which is whole wheat flour. Lots of Basmati rice. I was scolded as I watched him rinse his rice several times, because I told him I just throw it in the sauce pan with water before I cook it. "No, Darling, must always rinse rice. Think of where it comes from, in fields, and lays out and gets dust on it and other things. You must always wash several times until the water is clear." Good lesson.

He also uses a lot of yogurt in his dishes. He prefers Indian yogurt, but Greek yogurt is very similar and a great substitute.

Dessert, if he indulges, is fresh fruit. Red wine sparingly.

In the late evening before bedtime he will have tea with crackers or a biscuit, which might be a shortbread cookie or a simple cookie.

Our sumptuous meal at Daniel's house that Bali prepared during my initial interview, was lamb curry, cucumber salad, and steamed rice. Since many things are discussed at the dinner table, I kept a recorder going while we ate and conversed with Bali about his life. Throughout the recording are many "Ohhhhs" and "Ahhhhs", and "Oh, this is sooo good" as utensils tinkled against our plates while we went for another bite. Had we had a baby in the room, I am sure it would have been charmed by the sounds.

I have included those recipes and some others that Bali and I talked about. My husband Dan, our son Daniel, and our younger son David all love to cook. Kim, my daughter, who drove to Bend from Portland so I could introduce her to Bali, isn't driven by food menus and homemade cooking as the rest of us. She did, however, fall in love with Bali and vice versa.

Cucumber Riata

I teaspoon cumin seed
I tablespoon cooking oil (virgin olive oil)
½ cup to I cup fresh cilantro, chopped with stems
I large tomato, quartered or chopped?
I cucumber , peeled, sliced and seeded
½ teaspoon salt (optional)
½ red onion, sliced or 4 scallions stems
I Serrano pepper with seeds (I removed seeds in spite of the fact it was not the Indian way)
8 oz Greek Yogurt if you can't get Indian Yogurt

I.   Heat oil in skillet until hot and add the cumin seeds until they black, about I minute on medium high heat.
2.   Mix tomatoes, cucumber, onions, cilantro, and pepper in a bowl. Add yogurt and mix.
3.   Add the oil and cumin seeds. Mix well. Chill.

Lamb Curry
(from the NY Times Recipe)

½ cup cooking oil
1 onion, quartered and sliced
3 large cloves garlic, finely chopped
1 tablespoon finely chopped fresh ginger root
2 bay leaves, chopped
6 whole cloves
12 whole black peppercorns
1 ½ inch pieces of whole cinnamon stick
6 cherry tomatoes, halved, or two tomatoes, quartered
4 ½ tablespoons imported Madras-style curry powder
1 ½ teaspoons turmeric
1 tablespoon paprika
¼ cup water
3 pounds boneless lamb cubes, cut from the leg or shoulder
 1 ½ to 2 tablespoons salt

1.   Heat the oil in a heavy skillet or pan. Fry the onion in it until lightly brown; add garlic, ginger, bay leaves, cloves, peppercorns, cinnamon and tomatoes and cook 2 minutes.
2.   Mix the curry powder with the turmeric, paprika and water and add to the pan.
3.   Cook, stirring about 3 minutes over high heat, adding a tablespoon or two of water to prevent sticking if necessary.
4.   Add the meat and the salt and cook, stirring 1 minute. Cover and cook over medium heat about 30 minutes, or until the meat is tender. No liquid is added,

the liquid comes out of the meat to make the sauce as it cooks.

Bali used the basic recipe in *The New York Times* for Lamb Curry, but we used lamb chops and kept the bones attached, using the whole lamb chop. I duplicated this at home with pork chops.

Basmati & Other Rices

Daniel and Bali have rice cookers so they use them according to the directions and their rice comes out perfect. I don't use a rice cooker. Bought one and never seemed to work it properly, also, I use a lot of varieties of rice. On Okinawa, my mother and I were taught this: A lady, who could not speak English well, held up her index finger and pointed to the top joint, and said, "This much rice." She pointed to the second joint and said, "This much water." Bottom line, for brown rice I put in the ratio of two to one: one part rice, two parts water (usually 1 cup to 2 cups), bring to a boil, cover, and simmer on low for 45 minutes. I usually add Sesame oil while it simmers for Asian cooking.

White rice cooks faster and needs a bit less water. I do one cup rice and 1-¾ cups water, bring them to a boil, cover, and simmer 20 minutes. Bali said to always add butter to Basmati. "Don't forget to wash your rice, Darling."

Rice Palao

I black cardamom pod
I bay leaf
3" cinnamon stick
I teaspoon whole black pepper corns
I teaspoon whole cloves
I teaspoon cumin seeds
I cup uncooked rice
2 cups water
½ stick butter (I/4 cup)
Salt to personal taste
½ cup green peas

I.   Heat butter in a heavy skillet and all the spices until they turn black but don't burn. Add the rice, 2 cups water, salt, and peas.
2.   Bring to a boil and reduce heat to simmer for 20 minutes.

Andrew, Bali's son, asked for his father's tea recipe. It was always presented as an ancient recipe, which we might consider as Chai Tea, and it helps with colds and congestion besides being soothing and delicious.

Bali Ram's Nepalese Tea

4 cups water
I cup milk
I cinnamon stick
4 white cardamom pods
I" fresh ginger, smashed
I tea bag (Lipton black tea)
Sugar to taste

1.   Bring water, spices and tea and boil for 5 minutes in a small pot.
2.   Remove from heat and add milk and dissolve sugar to taste. Serve hot and store leftover tea in the refrigerator.

A Recent Visit to India

Photo by Daniel Biggs, Jr. in Bend, Oregon, U.S.A.

The British admired Indian culture, however, when Bali was young, the indigenous people were not allowed in the British social clubs and public houses, such as the

New Empire Theater, the hall in which Bali performed for Mother Teresa. Bali and governor were the first Indians allowed there. He said, "Indians couldn't even look at the theater or the Brits would beat the shit out them. Brits could take Indian wives or female friends, but no Indian men were allowed. They couldn't go into offices, clubs, British homes or bathrooms. They couldn't piss in the same bath hole."

Bali recalled the opulence of the steps, columns, and the lobby being white marble with red carpet on the inside of the New Empire Theater. He described it as looking like a temple with a capacity of thousands of people. It was the place the British went for parties and large functions. He remembered memorial gardens with a statue of Queen Victoria. People stood in line for hours to see the painting inside depicting the history of Calcutta.

In a recent visit to India, Bali was very saddened by the dramatic changes to the country, and said, "What happened to this place?" because it had changed so much. He said that the New Empire hall and the Light House are on Chowringhee Street and both are movie theaters now. They were next to the Albright Hotel which must have been renamed, as I am unable to locate it by the name at this time.

Half of all the musicians that Bali had toured with have died by now. "I go through my life like a rainbow. I was at the top of the world and now I'm at the bottom of my career, but at the same time I had a very nice life that everybody should have. For the way I've been treated and my beautiful experiences, I give thanks to Desmond Doig." He began to choke up when he continued, "I miss him so much. He was the one with the vision. He saw who I was and he helped me with it. It was incredible." He thought that Doig had died just a couple of years ago, but he died in 1983. For Bali the loss of his dear mentor and friend is still raw, as though it just happened. Doig is buried in the Embassy in Kathmandu, having died at age 63.

Bali became an American citizen; however, his entire life has been honoring his origins of Nepal and India as a world-wide goodwill ambassador, through his religion, his dress, music, and dance. Preparing, sharing, and teaching the cuisines of India and Nepal are evidenced through his cooking classes and dining with friends. He remains respectful of the customs and mythology. He has lifetime friends in India and visits as often as he is able. His heart is still there and so is his goodwill.

He danced in India in 2012, and they loved him and wouldn't even let him off the stage. He is still very popular there. We feel that India will embrace his biography and honor a great elder who represented their country and Nepal with grace and dignity and shared the culture of classical Indian dancing worldwide

"Life is very precious. Very, very precious and it's also an illusion. You think it is reality, but we are living an illusion. Nobody seems to know what reality is. We are here for a very short time, actually, and I didn't realize the brain I have now if I had it about 50 years ago, I would have everything."

Bali said, "You know, I met so many celebrities, so many people and I was so ignorant of not knowing who they were. It like ignorant is bliss."

"Well, I see you as being innocent, from another country, and focused on your art."

"Yeah, I know I was. I didn't even know Mahatma Gandhi when I tried to steal his stick and run. That era was a golden era for me. I met all the leaders, the famous ones: Mahatma Gandhi, Mother Teresa, Martin Luther King, Jr., John D. Rockefeller III, President Kennedy, Haile Salessie, Picasso. So many." At the time he had no idea how important those people were or that he was walking in the footprints of major, historical events.

He always ends our conversations with, "I love you," and I always return with, "I love you, too."

When he sometimes has a tough time in life, when he is a bit down and lonely, he said, "It's like a dream passing through my eyes. All the people I have met. All the things I have done. All the happiness and the sadness I have. I have really enjoyed life. I met so many people, dignitaries…I don't believe that it all happened, but it happened. It like a dream, and I am here in Bend working at McMenamins," and he laughed heartily. "Yesterday I was very distressed because they cutting my hours."

He thought back about his marriage and children. "One baby happen and we were very happy, the second baby, she got pregnant and she didn't want anything to do with me anymore," and he could not understand that. He thought Amy would be his lifetime partner. "I loved her very, very much. This was the first time I really, really enjoyed another person into my heart and it was sincere. A lot of women said to me 'I give you this much money. I just want to have a baby with you.' I said no!"

Bali confided to me recently, "I could have never married her without selling the ranch because I was able to live on the money for some time, but that was a long time ago. Today I am absolutely destitute, living in Bend as prep cook, with my hours cut back to two days a week."

Bali Ram at age 77
Photo by Daniel Biggs, Jr.

Epilogue

I called Bali in early October, 2012, as I do at least weekly, and I told him one of my dreams in writing about his life was to reunite him with his estranged daughter, Shamina. I knew that she would turn 18 in September and September had just ended, bringing the chilly October nights of our true four seasons.

Bali picked up his cell phone a week ago. "Hello."

"Daddy?"

He said, "Who's this?"

"It's Shamina."

"Shamina, my dear. My darling baby. How sweet your voice is," and it had been about 10 years since he had heard that voice.

"I might be coming out with Andrew to see you."

"That would be great, Honey. It would be the greatest gift *ever* I received in my life."

Bali told me, "Shamina means 'of the light,' the rainbow that forms on the oil lamp. If you light an oil lamp, it gives a little blue rainbow. That's my Shamina." He said he had tears in his eyes and he started shaking.

"Daddy, I'd like to see you again."

"Well, it's about time because Daddy getting very old. You never know when I am gone."

She was very happy to talk to him directly. My dream came true for one mission for this book, to reunite Bali with his daughter. I hung up the phone and did the "ugly cry," sobbing for two or three minutes.

My husband Dan was on the lap top opposite me and just shook his head, knowing I wouldn't be able to talk about it for a while.

And so the Golden Book of Bali Ram's life has closed for now, but it is far from over. He envisioned his story ending, still sitting by the lazy river. While he sat there with his lovely daughter by his side, a tall, handsome young man named Andrew was behind them, listening to the stories of his father's wondrous life. Bali put his in hand in the water and the ripples went into the river and moved with the current, as this chapter of his life's story came to an end. He closed the Golden Book.

Since he is still performing without being winded, I am confident that there will be many more performances for this talented, loving, sweet man. Is he a bit vain? Just a little, and deservedly so. I am confident that he will be honored and cherished by people around the world. I am confident that he will dance on grand stages again with the audience cheering and standing for him and yelling, "Bravo, Bali Ram! He really is Rhythm by Nature."

About the Author

Terrie Biggs has been writing creative non-fictional novels for years. Her first published book is *One of Eleven: Based on the Life of Gary Kopperud.* She is working on a collection of letters her great-grandfather wrote to his new bride in the Civil War, *Letters from Gil.* Her first book is based on the first two American women to settle in the Oregon "country" and will be available by early 2014. Terrie resides in La Grande, Oregon, with her husband Dan. Their children are adults. She has a lifetime passion for kitchen design, and owns her own business.

Check out her books at
http://www.novelsbyterrie.com

20152522R00118

Made in the USA
Charleston, SC
27 June 2013